FROM OOPS TO AHA

FROM OOPS TO AHA

Portraits of Learning From Mistakes in Kindergarten

Maleka Donaldson

ROWMAN & LITTLEFIELD
Lanham • Boulder • New York • London

Published by Rowman & Littlefield
An imprint of The Rowman & Littlefield Publishing Group, Inc.
4501 Forbes Boulevard, Suite 200, Lanham, Maryland 20706
www.rowman.com

6 Tinworth Street, London SE11 5AL, United Kingdom

British Library Cataloguing in Publication Information Available

Library of Congress Cataloging-in-Publication Data

Names: Donaldson, Maleka, 1980- author.
Title: From oops to aha : portraits of learning from mistakes in kindergarten / Maleka Donaldson.
Other titles: Portraits of learning from mistakes in kindergarten
Description: Lanham, Maryland : Rowman & Littlefield, 2021.
Identifiers: LCCN 2020056591 (print) | LCCN 2020056592 (ebook) | ISBN 9781475857016 (cloth) |
    ISBN 9781475857023 (paperback) | ISBN 9781475857030 (epub)
Subjects: LCSH: Kindergarten. | Teacher-student relationships. | Interaction analysis in education.
Classification: LCC LB1169 .D66 2021 (print) | LCC LB1169 (ebook) | DDC 372.21/8--dc23
LC record available at https://lccn.loc.gov/2020056591
LC ebook record available at https://lccn.loc.gov/2020056592

For my mother, Cynthia,
whose support has made everything possible in my life

For my uncle, Keith,
whose memory reminds me to seek the good
in everything

And for my daughter, Naomi,
who daily inspires me to be my best

CONTENTS

PREFACE

My obsession with mistakes is firmly anchored in my life in the classroom. As a kindergarten teacher, I experienced firsthand the extent to which contextual factors shaped my instructional practice—a reality that profoundly influenced how and how often I could offer my students feedback and opportunities to learn from their mistakes.

I first taught kindergarten in the heart of Washington, DC, serving an almost 100 percent African American student population. I was elated to be hired into this position—it was a dream come true because I wanted to teach the age level and I was eager to serve children like me, children who grew up in the inner city. Although my passion for kindergarten didn't fade, I was quickly worn thin by the extent to which the factors around me constrained my teaching. Standard classroom resources were in short supply, so I spent my own money—hundreds of dollars—purchasing the basic school supplies that I needed to do my job properly. When I went to the copy machine—which was routinely out of order—I always brought along my own paper, from a personal stash in my locked supply closet. The manipulatives and books specified in the provided curriculum were often missing or insufficient, making it difficult to enact lessons properly. I had no toys or games for the children to play with during free time or indoor recess, and I did not have construction paper for basic art projects until January after a Christmas donation from a local organization.

My teaching assistant was constantly removed from my class without prior notice and reassigned to cover other rooms when fellow teachers called in sick. At the same time, despite a dearth of resources, I felt tremendous pressure from my principal to get the children to achieve. My challenge was compounded by the fact that I had a large class with a number of children with extreme behavioral issues for which I did not receive a lot of administrative support. At the end of the day, I did the best that I could under the circumstances and with the resources that I had. I tried to meet the children where they were to challenge them and to keep them engaged with learning. By the close of the academic year, I still felt strongly that I wanted to remain a kindergarten teacher but was discouraged by the many hurdles I faced at that school.

A couple of years later, I got a job teaching at a Los Angeles school that offered me an extremely well-resourced kindergarten classroom. There were rows of shelves containing every manipulative I could dream of; a large supply closet full of more materials than I could possibly use in a year (or even a couple of years); and brand new top-of-the-line curriculum, workbooks, and accompanying materials for my students and me to use. An extremely small class size, combined with having an aide consistently present and active during our intensive instructional times, allowed me to have frequent and substantive feedback interactions.

This set of circumstances facilitated my ability to provide strong, supportive, and individualized instruction for each student. I typically gave every single child corrective feedback and individual one-on-one check-ins on a daily basis. Although my Los Angeles kindergarten classroom had many affordances by comparison to my prior experience in DC, my job was still no cakewalk. It was very taxing and required considerable effort to balance all the children's various needs. But I was able to focus intently on lesson planning, classroom management, and meeting the children's social and emotional needs because I did not have to worry about whether I had whiteboard markers or copy paper, whether my aide would unexpectedly be pulled out of my class, or whether my planning period would be cancelled at the last minute because the PE teacher called in sick.

In this space, I had a principal who always had my back when different issues arose, little achievement pressure, and the autonomy to be a professional. These small assurances provided a stable work environment where I was set up for success and could thrive in my profession. It afforded the means for me to be my personal best, rather than simply to survive another day.

My life as a kindergarten teacher—and particularly these two contrasting experiences—has motivated all of my subsequent work as a teacher–educator and as a researcher. Although my skills, passion, and core values as a teacher remained consistent, I found that being embedded in these disparate environments led to two wildly different classroom experiences and the realization that not all kindergarten classrooms are equal. I am not sure that others who have not had an experience like this can really understand the power of this discrepancy.

I was the same person all along but, because of many factors outside of my control, I could not be the same teacher across the two contexts. With fewer students, each child received more one-on-one attention. With consistent staff support, I could reliably execute differentiated instruction and check in with individual students regularly. With ample tangible resources on hand, I could prepare and execute lessons with greater ease. With fewer pressures to attain proficiency, I could be more patient; and we could meander through our learning experience, adjusting the pace as needed. In both settings, the underlying challenge of the teaching itself was still the same—I had myriad personalities, varied learning needs, and a diverse set of learning trajectories in every subject that I taught. But with resources, I was able to serve those needs better.

Variations across school settings dictate how teachers approach instruction, including how they respond to mistakes. But, even within a single classroom, different children's perceptions of mistakes and feedback can vary significantly. My earliest curiosity about mistakes and student-teacher feedback interactions piqued when I made a perplexing observation as I taught writing to two particular little girls—"Emma" and "Joelle"—in my Los Angeles classroom. Writing is one of my favorite things to teach kindergarteners; in my classroom, the children practiced free writing constantly. Emma was a small girl and almost five years old when she first arrived in my class. I still remember her bright smile, tiny sing-song voice, and wide black curls that easily fell down her back and swung as she moved. During writing practice, Emma would constantly ask me how to spell various words. Because at the time I was more interested in building her confidence and getting her ideas on paper, I initially indulged her request for spellings of a few difficult words that she wanted to use. As I would call out the letters, one by one, she would carefully print each one on the page. But eventually, it was clear that she was ready to take the next brave step to apply her knowledge of letter sounds and spell out all of the words on her own, even the more irregular and unconventional ones.

At first, Emma was a little nervous, but I enthusiastically assured her that I believed in her knowledge of letter sounds. I could tell that she had the underlying skills needed to spell out the unknown and did not need me. For this task it did not matter to me whether she was exactly right, but that she tried her very best. This gentle nudge was all Emma needed to set her on her way. She dove into invented spelling, which allowed her to happily (and independently) string together any words she wanted into sentences and stories. Through gentle but immediate corrective feedback on her completed writings, I helped Emma gradually learn the "grown-up spellings" for a great number of words. But, in the meantime, the quest for correct spelling did not impede Emma's creativity nor curb her confidence as a writer. By giving Emma permission to make mistakes, I freed her to write anything she wanted. Over days, weeks, and months, her one sentence picture captions gradually grew to multi-page sagas, and both her writing and reading skills skyrocketed.

I also taught Joelle in the same school. When she entered my class, she was a few months older (and a few inches taller) than Emma, and a bit shy and reserved. Joelle started the year with very impressive reading skills, but it did not take long for me to notice that she had a strong aversion to making mistakes. Writing was a big challenge for Joelle; she often struggled to get anything on the page because she wanted all the spellings to be exactly right every time.

This is not an expectation I conveyed to her; actually, it was quite the opposite. But even when I assured Joelle, just as I did for Emma, that the focus was on developing our stories, that what mattered was that she try her best, and that I didn't care whether she spelled it right or wrong, she was still not willing to take that risk. Many times, she struggled to get something—anything—on the page, and her progress in this area flatlined for a long while, despite my coaching and positive encouragement. I remember at one point she even asked me, "Can I have an easier work?" with the hopes that she could flex her smarts and complete it correctly and quickly, without mistakes. Reflecting on the experience of teaching these two kindergarteners, I found it absolutely fascinating that with the same teacher and within the same kindergarten setting, two children could have such different reactions to their own mistakes and to trying something new. On one hand, once she got past her initial hesitations,

Emma didn't seem phased by mistakes. On the other hand, Joelle was completely frozen and her fear of making mistakes held back her engagement in our learning and her individual academic growth.

Beyond the fact that there is incredible variation in children's skill levels, personalities, attitudes, maturity, and the like, teaching takes place in a specific context with its own range of variables. No doubt, teachers need to know how to respond to children's mistakes, misunderstandings, and confusions in ways that foster learning and engagement—and across a number of domains. Layered atop that are structural factors built into the fiber of the classroom and school. How frequently teachers give children feedback is a factor of time; packed school schedules curtail how often a teacher, an aide, or other adults can invest in the effort. Lesson pacing aligns with state standards, district-wide policies, and expectations around achievement test performance. The lessons—both content and quality—are determined by the curricular resources provided to teachers, training and professional development, as well as the tangible resources at the teacher's disposal—be that paper, pencils, art supplies, whiteboard markers, copy machine access, lamination machines, tape, and more.

Given that children can vary within one classroom setting as widely as Emma and Joelle, and that schools can vary as widely as my DC and LA classrooms, there is a lot to consider. In this book, I seek to explore the wide range of opportunities that U.S. kindergarten children are offered to learn from mistakes and to receive feedback from their teachers in real-world contexts.

INTRODUCTION

Pulling back the curtain on mistakes in kindergarten intrigues me for a number of reasons. First, my foundational reason is that everyone—in kindergarten and at all ages—necessarily makes mistakes when learning something new. When I first started looking at praise and feedback, I found a plethora of laboratory-based research that explores the impact of feedback on learning. From brain scans to structured interventions to eye-tracking studies, the consensus was pretty clear: corrective feedback and trial-and-error practice are absolutely critical when learning something new. To learn from mistakes and misunderstandings, learners of all ages need time and space to work with new material, as well as scaffolding, support, and corrective feedback. These insights make perfect sense within a kindergarten classroom, where children tackle an array of new skills across many developmental arenas and constantly make mistakes.

Second, I am fascinated by the relational spaces in which mistakes are corrected. We know from a variety of theorists in human development and psychology that people learn in a social context and that interpersonal and environmental factors shape how we navigate life and learning. The very act of providing feedback—including our words, body language, and prior history with the person and content—is a social exchange that is anchored in the ecology of our learning space. When undergirded by a basis of trust, feedback can be received as a mark of care, concern, and loving attention. For example, as a writer, I lean into the editorial comments of trusted friends and colleagues who I know have a vested interest in my work. I trust that they not only believe in my potential for future success but are also able to provide critical feedback to push me to refine my work and help me consider alternative perspectives. But when correction comes from a source with whom a steady rapport has not been established, it can hint of judgment and hinder my learning from blunders and missteps as I try to posture and hide evidence of the mistakes ever having happened. This reminds me of rejections and harsh critiques I have received from distant reviewers who may have valid suggestions that could help me refine my writing, but the delivery of their feedback is shrouded in an opaque review process. Hence, as compared to friendly feedback from supportive colleagues, article rejections from critical reviewers sting a bit more and rile up insecurities about my abilities—even if the substance of the feedback is similar in content. The same is true of student-teacher relationships in the classroom. With trust and connectedness, teachers are positioned to help children receive and leverage corrective feedback that can support skill development and personal growth.

Third, I have come to understand that the potential to learn from mistakes is dependent on perceptions and beliefs about our own abilities. This arises when we think of Carol Dweck's concept of a growth mindset—in which learners believe that hard work and effort can expand their intelligence, despite failures they may encounter along the way. In this sense, how we view our own personal ability impacts the actions that we are willing to take in our approach to learning. While, ideally, we hope to have a growth mindset in which our response to mistakes is *always* to exert more effort, the truth is that, for children and adults alike, this is rarely the case. Inevitably, there are at least few aspects of our lives for which we have a fixed mindset, believing that our intelligence is set and there is nothing we can do to improve it. Fortunately, our fixed mindsets can be changed to growth mindsets through interventions and experience. I think most teachers seek to set children up to expect mistakes, to be open to feedback for improvement, and to have adaptive responses to mistakes when they happen that allow them to continue to move forward with their learning.

And lastly, and perhaps most importantly, I have both lived and observed the fact that the way teachers respond to mistakes is not universally the same from one classroom to the next. Responses and expectations vary by school philosophy, curriculum, teacher, and, unfortunately, resource level. We are in a moment where we already know there are immense opportunity gaps in the United States that have real-world impact on children, with the most negative circumstances affecting those with the fewest financial resources and children of color. Instructional supports, tangible supplies, and resources in the classroom, along with teacher quality and training, all have an impact on the learning that goes on in the classroom, including how much and how quickly children learn. But these factors also impact the mistake culture of the learning environment. For example, if a classroom aide is only available part-time, that can limit when and how a kindergarten teacher can have individual conferences for Writer's Workshop; gather small groups for intensive intervention to practice skills; or sit with students one on one to scaffold a challenging piece of work they are puzzling through. The ability to provide corrective feedback depends on the structure of the curriculum, expectations of the district, autonomy afforded to the teacher, and supplies and supports at their disposal.

Within this book, I present portraits of the day-to-day experiences of four public-school teachers and their kindergarten students, offering snapshots of what teaching and learning from mistakes looks like in their classrooms. This book extends two bodies of existing scholarly work related to this topic: (1) lab-based studies—mostly in psychology—that establish how and to what extent corrective feedback and praise impact learning, and (2) educational research that examines the role that student-teacher relationships, emotion, and human interaction play in learning—from mistakes or otherwise. By offering a rare glimpse into the real-world experiences that kindergarteners and their teachers have while learning from mistakes, I uncover new pathways of usable knowledge that can inform a variety of stakeholders interested in instructional practices in early childhood education, learning from feedback and mistakes, and more.

Each chapter is a portrait of the various ways that one particular teacher responds to mistakes, in context. I carefully selected and invited the participating teachers—established veteran educators who excelled within their schools and showed an eagerness to consider the role of mistakes in their own practice. I also wanted the group of teachers to reflect disparate school settings, as a demonstration and exploration of the extent to which teachers' responses can vary, in context. I spent substantial time with each teacher—between forty to seventy hours at each school site—as I video-recorded all instruction and interviewed them on multiple occasions. Later, I pored over these data for hundreds of hours to discern patterns within and across these four U.S. kindergarten settings. Employing Sara Lawrence-Lightfoot's method of portraiture, I crafted detailed vignettes that illustrate the various strategies that the teachers use to provide corrective feedback—pushing, encouraging, redirecting, and otherwise steering students in various directions with their learning. [*Note*: The names of all teachers, children, and schools have been changed to protect their identities.] Juxtaposing these cases puts their differences into sharp contrast. Rather than simply providing a distilled list of best practices or positioning the teachers as ideal types that we should emulate, I choose instead to focus on revealing just how messy and complex the work of teaching young children can be and how anchored the learning endeavor is in our humanity.

I start with an account of Mr. Allen, who teaches in a diverse, urban public school. Daily, he manages the constrained resources of time, materials, and support, as well as heavy pressure to meet district benchmarks and complete a litany of standardized assessments. In this context, he works diligently to help students improve their academic abilities, including basic alphabet identification, writing, drawing, and math skills. He frequently tells children "kiss your brain" when they are right, helps them to correct themselves when they make mistakes, and expects them to do their "*best* best job"—holding them accountable to their own prior performance. Depending on the circumstance, he sometimes pushes students to focus squarely on the facts; at other moments, he entertains guesses. Within a context of limited resources and support, combined with high achievement pressure, Mr. Allen struggles to help students correct their mistakes quickly and gain the independence needed for success in first grade.

Next, I turn to Ms. Rivers, who teaches kindergarten in an urban public charter school that predominantly enrolls Black and Latinx students. In fulfillment of the school's mission, she focuses intently on pushing young children to achieve at the highest levels possible, regardless of individual personality, learning style, or family attributes. Ms. Rivers is fastidious in monitoring the use of class time. She ensures that they sit at attention silently and transition seamlessly from one whole-group activity to the next, thereby working individually to advance collective learning. Mistakes are quickly called out and discarded. She wants all children to land on correct answers quickly and efficiently, does not accept any partially correct responses, and expects confidence when students speak in class. While acknowledging that young children are not well practiced at discussion, Ms. Rivers feels this is a critically important skill they will need for their future academic success and provides constant feedback and redirection about how to appropriately engage in classroom conversations.

In the third chapter, I enter a public Montessori classroom with Miss Carrie, who invests hours a day providing individual feedback to her students. Every morning, children engage in long blocks of independent work time during which they complete learning activities by themselves or with one partner. The teacher expects that children select and remain focused on appropriate tasks, and that they should interact with her and others with respect and kindness. When it comes to mistakes, children check their own work with self-correcting Montessori materials. Then— if needed—they have extended, open conversations with their teacher to help them land on the right answer before moving on to the next project. Miss Carrie is direct in telling students when they are wrong, while simultaneously warm, patient, and enduring as she asks guiding questions to help them correct their own mistakes without giving away the right answer. The children in Miss Carrie's class own the mistake-correction process, and she positions herself in a supporting role as they drive their personal learning.

And finally, the fourth portrait features a teacher working in a well-resourced, suburban public school in a predominantly White neighborhood. Mrs. Tucker's classroom is a space in which students are provided ample opportunities to learn from their mistakes, with plenty of time devoted to practice and teacher feedback. She works to make kindergarten a flexible "gray area" in which children can try new things, self-correct, and propel their own learning. At the same time, she pushes them toward improved performance, differentiating expectations depending on each student's capabilities. Mrs. Tucker frequently features mistakes during classroom instruction, whether it is asking students to correct errors during a game or handout as a part of skills practice, or by excitedly—and publicly—discussing a "fantastic oops" made by a student during a whole-group lesson.

Teaching kindergarten students was one of the most meaningful roles I have held in my career. I believed in them, invested in them, and also set them on a trajectory toward future success in upper grades by providing a solid early foundation. Kindergarten sets the tone for children's future academic lives. We need to take time to really attend to the relationship- and interaction-based moments of learning in early education. We need to take stock of how the subtlety of our words, body language, classroom rules, and interaction styles shape how children approach learning. And, most importantly, we must acknowledge that all kindergarten classrooms are not the same. Kindergarten teaching is challenging work and has as many, if not more, demands as any other grade. With benchmarks and standards increasingly driving curriculum and classroom expectations, we must consider how early childhood education is shifting, and that recent changes may not be universally beneficial and definitely not uni- formly manifested across settings. The stories of how these four kinder- garten teachers respond to children's mistakes can help us see what is happening in the small moments of teaching—individual interactions be- tween humans—in detail and in context.

1

MR. ALLEN

Transforming Mistakes into Melodies

Mr. Allen's class meeting always starts with a song.

Good morning, everyone!
Good morning; we're happy; we're here!

It is January and by this point, midway through the school year, Mr. Allen has clearly established that this tune signals the beginning of their daily class meeting. When he starts a cappella in his loud and strong tenor voice, the students quickly join him in chorus. He sings the short, peppy jingle with a tone of enthusiasm, matched by his bright, brown eyes and a full, genuine, and friendly smile. Mr. Allen is a White man of medium height; his brown, wavy hair is cut short and swept to the side. Today, he is wearing a long-sleeved striped sweater with alternating black, brown, orange, and cream-colored horizontal stripes, paired with khaki pants and black dress shoes. At the front of his class, he looks both professional and comfortable as he starts the work of the day.

The students are seated "criss-cross banana sauce" in their assigned spots on the rug in the class library. Looking across the room, I see little faces of every hue, and hair of every color, length, and texture. Each child occupies one of the brightly colored squares delineated by perpendicular lines on the rug. Once the short song ends, Mr. Allen begins the class's routine series of daily check-ins and songs.

"What's wrong with the calendar?"

All across the area rug in the library, many small hands shoot up into the air. With a pensive look on his face, his eyes scan the room.

"Angelo," he calls.

"You have to change it to the twenty-seventh," Angelo replies.

"To the twenty-seventh," echoes Mr. Allen. With that, he stands, carefully steps the short distance from his chair over to the calendar and moves the clip to the proper spot.

"Who knows what day of the week it is?" He calls on Scott.

"Ummm. Wednesday."

"Today *is* Wednesday," echoes Mr. Allen. "What *was* yesterday, Arthur?"

"Tuesday," Arthur quickly replies.

"And if yesterday *was* Tuesday," Mr. Allen continues, "and today *is* Wednesday, what day *will* tomorrow be, Alyse?"

"Thursday," she responds. As each of the three students offers a reply to his questions, he captures their responses on a printed sign atop the whiteboard at the front of the class for all to see.

After Alyse's answer, the chart is fully updated, and Mr. Allen immediately breaks into song. "*Days of the week*" . . . click click. "*Days of the week*" . . . click click. "*Days of the week, days of the week, days of the week*" . . . click click.

To the tune of "The Addams Family," the students collectively sing and click their tongues along with him. As they sing the verse of the song, Mr. Allen stands next to the calendar and points to each day name, in turn.

"*There's Sunday then there's Monday. There's Tuesday then there's Wednesday. There's Thursday then there's Friday. And then there's Saturday. Days of the week*" . . . click click. "*Days of the week*" . . . click click. "*Days of the week, days of the week, days of the week*" . . . click click.

As they finish that song, without pause, the class immediately breaks into "Happy Days," the next tune in their sequence.

"*Sunday, Monday, happy days! Tuesday, Wednesday, happy days! Thursday, Friday, happy days! Saturday. What a day! Groovin' all week with you . . .*"

The children sing and do hand motions throughout the song. When it ends, Mr. Allen clasps his hands together and sings the question, "*What is today's date?*"—repeating a single note in an energetic and comically dramatic tone. With his hands in his pockets, he sings, in that same single note, *"Kameron, I love your school listening look. You're making me very proud of you, and I love how you're always trying your best!"* As he finishes his brief serenade, Mr. Allen raises his left hand, swinging his open palm toward the calendar, inviting Kameron to offer the full date aloud to the class.

The room is silent. Kameron is turned toward Mr. Allen and leaning forward on his hands from his spot on the rug, placed just behind his twin brother, Kevin. Today, as every day I have been in the classroom, the two boys completely match each other, clothed in identical, red, collared shirts—their black, straight, shiny hair styled in trendy, short-angled bob haircuts. Kameron rocks as he replies, shifting the weight of his body backward and forward onto his hands. As he moves in the silence, Kameron states each part of the date a moment or two after Mr. Allen points at the placement of each answer on the calendar. "Wednesday. January. 27." Kameron takes his time and, with Mr. Allen's nonverbal help pointing to the class calendar, he correctly states the day of the week, month, and date.

"Nice work, Kameron." Mr. Allen applauds his success, rapidly clapping his hands together five times. "You were thinking really hard. Alyse!"

Alyse takes her turn and, again, Mr. Allen points to each place on the calendar as she speaks. In a mild voice, she quickly says her response. "Today is Wednesday, January 27."

Mr. Allen's eyes widen slightly, and he does a quick nod of his head. "Alyse, you are getting faster and faster at that. Olivia, wanna give it a go?" As he did for the other students, he stretches his hand out toward the calendar, resting his pointer finger on the word *Wednesday* on the chart. He stands there, smiling and pointing, waiting for her response.

After a brief pause, Olivia admits, "I don't remember."

"So, let's say it," offers Mr. Allen immediately. "If we forget what day of the week it is, we start at the beginning. So, what is this one?" He points to the word *Sunday* on the classroom calendar. "It's always . . ."

With this open-ended invitation, Olivia speaks up, reciting each word as Mr. Allen points to it on the chart. "Sunday, Monday, Tuesday . . ." She pauses for a quick second—"Wednesday!" Olivia stops and looks up at Mr. Allen.

"Wednesday," he echoes back, affirming the answer she has reached using his strategy. In acknowledgment of her making this connection, he extends one arm toward the correct answer on the calendar, and reaches the other toward little Olivia, who has just provided the word.

He moves on, pointing to the month at the top of the calendar. Olivia immediately says, "January." He points to the twenty-seven. "Seven," she says, making an attempt to read the day of the month he is pointing at.

"Twenty-seven," he says in a pleasant voice and with a single nod of the head.

"Twenty-seven," she echoes.

In these exchanges, I sense a level of ease and comfort between Mr. Allen and the students when answering in front of the class. These interactions about identifying the date illustrate the general approach Mr. Allen takes to instruction in his classroom. In small and large group settings, I watch as he gives many different children opportunities to try—and to shine. He scaffolds learning so that students can avoid mistakes, proactively drawing attention to where they can find the right answer (when there is one). He also thoroughly encourages them when they do make mistakes and praises them when they succeed. In his praise, he highlights Kameron's effort level and Alyse's improvement over time. And when Olivia isn't able to put together the answer on her own, he talks her through concrete strategies that can help her use the calendar in front of her to find the right answer for herself.

STRUM WHAT YOU'VE GOT: STRIVING TO MAKE THE MOST OF THE LESS THAN IDEAL

Shaun Allen has taught kindergarten at Prince Elementary for nine years. He started at the school with a newly minted college degree in early childhood education and several teaching certifications. In his self-described "traditional kindergarten," he works with twenty-three five- and six-year-old students Monday through Friday, for a full, six-hour day. Many of the students come to school on buses or attend before- and after-school programs while parents are at work. Reflective of the community served by the school, his class this year, and every year, is extremely diverse. Students have a wide array of family backgrounds and countries of origin that span four continents—Africa, Asia, Europe, and North America.

When seeking to understand how and why Mr. Allen responds to his students' mistakes in the way that he does, it is first necessary to consider the environment in which he teaches. Mr. Allen enjoys the reputation of being an excellent teacher and is a teacher-leader at Prince. For years, he has taken on roles above and beyond his classroom teaching, like leading his grade-level team, mentoring novice teachers who join the staff, and guiding initiatives on the school's Data Team—a group of staff members who analyze student data in search of ways to help teachers improve their work in the classroom.

In Mr. Allen's classroom, there are no worksheets. "When I look at a worksheet, it tells me maybe they knew the right answer and circled the right thing. Maybe they didn't; . . . maybe they guessed." He shares with me that during his training in college, he came to believe that worksheets offer very limited information about what students actually know. As a result of this philosophy, he largely engages in workshop-based teaching for reading, writing, and math in which, after a brief whole-group intro-duction, students engage in independent stations, doing work at their own pace. They rotate through various short activities when prompted, includ-ing one station in which Mr. Allen monitors their progress and gives individualized feedback when appropriate. In addition, each day, Mr. Allen has one or two designated forty-five-minute blocks of time set aside for work in a variety of classroom centers. His classroom is spa-cious and has several different centers students can choose from, includ-ing dramatic play, ABC table, the discovery table, block area, library, and the drawing table. Only a certain number of students are allowed to be in each space at a time, but once everyone has made their choices, the students can switch areas at their leisure as long as they move their cards on the centers chart to reflect the new location. While this is going on, Mr. Allen pulls small groups of students to the back of the room for instruction or interventions.

The children in Mr. Allen's classroom also spend one or two hours per day in whole-group instruction. This includes shared reading and the daily class meeting. It is during these times that students, with scaffolding from Mr. Allen, get opportunities to try out ideas, practice making story predictions, and offer their best guesses during classroom conversations with their teacher and peers.

After spending extended time in his classroom, I see that Mr. Allen works hard and he works well, but he also works within constraints all too familiar to many urban public-school teachers. The copy machine is old and finicky and, even when it does work, there is limited copy paper available. Mr. Allen does not like to give students handouts very often and much prefers to use whiteboards. However, whiteboard markers are a rare commodity, and he has to exert a fair amount of effort teaching the students to be gentle with them so they will last longer. He has one classroom aide—Mrs. Stanton—who helps him manage logistics in his classroom. However, because his union only mandates a part-time para-professional, there is a rule—either at the district or school level (he is unsure which level)—that he does not get a sub when she is out for sick days or vacation.

Although the classroom is big, the school building is old, and Mr. Allen constantly has to deal with issues related to its state of disrepair and inconvenient layout. When it rains, water seeps up from the floor. He places boxes from the lunchroom on the floor to help soak it up and to keep the children from sliding on the puddles. Once after a heavy rain, Diamond walks quickly from her table, slipping a little as the wet box shifts slightly under her foot. Mr. Allen calls out, "Watch the boxes, Diamond. I don't want you to get hurt." Bathroom and sink access is limited. Although there is a single bathroom just outside of their door, it has one stall and is shared among three or four classes; so, Mr. Allen's students only use it in case of emergency. Most often, the students line up and go all at once a few times a day, walking down to the cafeteria where there is a large girls' and boys' restroom. One of the classroom jobs is the "Clean Hands Helper," who brings a small basket containing the things the students will need to clean their hands—a bottle of hand sanitizer, a bottle of liquid soap, and a stack of brown paper towels cut in half. After they use the bathroom, they come out to get soap, go back in to wash, and then come back out to get a small towel before lining up to wait for classmates to finish. Mr. Allen frequently has to deal with mice, which I periodically witness darting across the floor during the day while the students are out of the room at lunch or at a class like gym or music. Recess time is limited, and the students only have one opportunity to go outside—after lunch at the end of the day, right before dismissal. Mr. Allen remarks that they simply go out at their assigned time so that they do not overlap with the older students in the school because it "would just be too many kids and not enough space" on the playground.

In addition to the issues he copes with in the school's infrastructure, the emotional burden of the needs of the students is sizable, particularly with this cohort of children. "In nine years, this is the hardest group because there's so many behaviors and all kinds of things going on. So, it's just . . . I'm tired every day . . . I feel like when I started, a few kids needed me more as a parent than a teacher. Everyone else just needed me to be their teacher. And then over the years, it's just completely switched. I'm like . . . I just can't be a good parent to twenty-three people. So, it's just . . . tiring." He laughs to himself. "Tryin' my best."

In response, I smile and say, "That's all you can do."

Beyond his dedication to teaching and overcoming the various challenges and resource constraints he faces in his classroom, Mr. Allen also enjoys and excels at music performance. His love of the arts is most tangibly reflected in his classroom by the presence of several musical instruments that reside in his room: a worn upright piano; a pale-yellow autoharp that lives on top of the piano; and an acoustic guitar with a light-colored wooden façade and a patterned shoulder strap. All three instruments are within easy reach of the large teacher's chair in the meeting area. When I ask, he shares with me that his instrument of choice is "definitely guitar, unless voice counts." This makes sense, as I see him strum the guitar and sing with the children almost every day that I visit his room. He shares with me that, years ago, he received the classroom guitar from a parent who had recently upgraded to a newer model. In his view, although the hand-me-down is "not in great shape," it still "sounds pretty decent." The guitar "lives at school," and I observe that it always sits by his side, ready for him to sing a song at a moment's notice.

Mr. Allen's use of the guitar in his class mirrors his approach to teaching and responding to mistakes in his kindergarten classroom. As a veteran teacher and as a guitar player, he strums the instruments available to him. He does not dwell on what he does *not* have but focuses on what he *has*. In his classroom guitar playing, he has an older instrument that is not ideal and does not provide the best sound. With a better instrument, he could produce a better sound, but this is what he has access to. Similarly, in his teaching, he does not necessarily work under ideal conditions, but he does his best to address students' mistakes and foster learning. He meets the students where they are and works to ensure the best outcome possible for each child within the resource and time constraints of his school. In the end, his skill, experience, and dedication allow him to create beautiful learning out of the limited resources available to him. That said, Mr. Allen has to manage many pressures, most notably requirements to complete assessments and to nudge student achievement toward rising kindergarten benchmarks.

PERFORMING UNDER PRESSURE: FACING THE FRUSTRATIONS OF ASSESSMENT AND ACHIEVEMENT EXPECTATIONS

As Mr. Allen describes it, mistakes are "just part of the learning process, right? If they weren't making mistakes, they wouldn't need my help." Just as one would expect a few wrong notes when first trying out a new musical piece, Mr. Allen expects wrong answers and misunderstandings as the children work toward the goal of meeting the district's grade-level performance standards. He explains to me that the vast majority of his students coming into kindergarten have had some sort of preschool experience, whether in one of the classrooms at Prince, in Head Start, or in other early learning programs in the area. These settings can vary widely in quality and rigor of academic focus, as well as the teaching philosophy that guides day-to-day classroom activities. Regardless of their background or the level at which they started, all students are expected to read at the same level by the close of the kindergarten year. There is a single, district-level standard despite the fact that Mr. Allen typically sees a huge variation in what different students can do coming into his class. Reflecting on the prior year, he recalls that he "had a kid who couldn't recognize their name in print, to a kid who started the year reading at a second-grade level." It is Mr. Allen's job to lead all students—even those entering with limited recognition of letter forms and corresponding sounds—to reading fluently by the start of first grade. A tradeoff of this heavy focus on reading is that he does not have the time or capacity to focus on correcting students' handwriting, which has no official standards. "I think, unless they go to the Catholic school, they don't have someone breathing down their neck about how to form letters." And so, in lieu of other skills for which he will be held accountable at the end of the year, he lets this go.

Despite his training and years of experience as an educator, his desire for small group and individualized instruction is often eclipsed by pressures to meet deadlines for various assessments he is required to complete. Mr. Allen has to administer seven different formal assessments over the course of the year. Each of these require him to test all of his students on a variety of skills, including letter identification, sound fluency, expressive vocabulary, kindergarten readiness skills (i.e., cutting, copying letters, jumping, fine motor, etc.), and reading level. With the exception of a few tasks on one of the tests, all seven must be given privately in a one-on-one administration. The most demanding test—for both student and teacher—seems to be the assessment for English Language Learners (ELL). Although he only has to administer it for a few students each year, it requires Mr. Allen to spend ninety minutes one on one with each child and has bubbles that the students have to fill in for themselves. This year he had to administer it to seven students, representing approximately ten-and-a-half hours of one-on-one time not focused on the whole class and also not focused on individual instruction.

Standardized assessment is a topic that Mr. Allen brings up frequently with me during the time I am in his class. Time and again, he expresses a great deal of frustration about the tests, both because of how long they take to administer, and because of how they are structured and scored. He is pressured to perform as a teacher so that his students uniformly reach or exceed a set cut score. Although there aren't specific consequences for not meeting benchmarks, he is expected to "have a certain number of students score proficient" on the test. In essence, this makes Mr. Allen responsible for decreasing the number of mistakes made by each student to a level deemed acceptable by the district.

In pursuing this goal, Mr. Allen finds it "really upsetting . . . that their progress is in no way considered." For example, on one of the tests focused on alphabet skills, he shows me an instance in which a student had "a 700 percent improvement," and another criterion on which the score almost tripled. In both cases, despite substantial increases in performance over the course of the year, the assessment rubric indicates that the student has failed. In Mr. Allen's view, the test does not adequately represent the amount of progress students make or the Herculean effort he puts forth to increase those skill levels. "I hate it. I think it's really unfair [because] . . . improvement is not in any way used to determine how they're doing. Kids who are above and beyond, there's no increased

expectation for them, and there's no scaled-back improvement expectation for kids who aren't meeting those standards." Mr. Allen finds it hard
to understand that despite the work he puts into helping the students
correct their misunderstandings and build skills, the expectations are such
that students who initially tested with lower levels of proficiency—but
demonstrate huge gains due to his direct interventions—still receive fail-
ing scores despite large leaps in their performance.

On another day, Mr. Allen shows me how a different assessment
works. It is a task during which students must read the words in order,
and their score is determined by how far they get without making mistakes. They can make up to four mistakes, and then that determines their
score. "The most frustrating thing about that reading test for me is that the
first time I give it, for most kids, there is not a single word they can do . . .
so, you stop at that level; . . . it's like basically 0 percent. . . . Some of the
kids, they'll go, they'll make a total of four errors and make *all* the other
words, but it is still considered less than [Level] A. . . . There's like, such
a difference between those two things." As he does the test with the
students and tracks their mistakes along the way, Mr. Allen observes that
getting *none* of the words right on the entire page counts for the exact
same score as getting *all* of the words on the page *except* the first four.
"What's frustrating is, like, there's no way to record it. It's just less than
90 percent."

Although Mr. Allen does not have control over the mandated assessments he must complete throughout the year, he has developed ways of
informally tracking student mistakes and milestones as a means to improve and tailor his instruction. He shows me a spreadsheet tracking
system he developed himself to record which uppercase and lowercase
letters each of the students recognized. He also has information about
progress in letter-sound knowledge. Despite the many formal assessments, there is not one that tracks this information, which is extremely
relevant to his work as a kindergarten teacher, according to Mr. Allen.

During assessments, students are not told what they got right or
wrong. Unlike workshops, centers, and other interventions that provide a
one-on-one interaction with the teacher with lots of comments and
prompts to improve their work, these tests do not offer students any real-
time feedback for improvement. And although the assessments often ask
Mr. Allen to count the number of mistakes made, the information is not
useful to him for instructional improvement. Instead, he explains that he

simply collects the data as instructed, computes the scores, and sends his reports off into "cyberspace," never to be seen or used again.

Despite his frustrations with the structure and demands of the assessments, Mr. Allen puts in a lot of effort to make the conditions the best that he can for the students when they are taking the tests. He has to put in some work to get the rest of the class to quietly engage in a second round of independent work and play at centers while he works one on one with students, either back at the table near the window or just outside the door in the hallway. The tests are often high stakes—the ELL test determines whether or not they will be in a regular classroom or sheltered English immersion in first grade, and establishes the level of interventions that will be provided—and he is fairly transparent with the students about just how important it is to be quiet.

One cold winter morning, they go over the day's schedule. Mr. Allen mentions to the class that they might have a "little extra centers at the end of the day . . . because I have to finish getting that test done as soon as possible so that we can get back to normal."

Later that day, just before they start the session, he again discusses the assessment. "I'm gonna be at the [back] table calling kids to work on tests, okay? So, if you need something, who do you need to talk to?"

The class calls out in response, "Mrs. Stanton," the aide in the classroom.

"Mrs. Stanton," he says, shaking his head from left to right, two or three times, looking out at the children. "I can't, I can't come look at something, even if you really want me to, so what I want you to do is take a picture with your brain and you can describe it to me later. Okay? And you can tell me about what you did." With this exchange, he clarifies with them the expectation about what they need to do when he is working one on one with a student doing the assessment. As an observer, I can clearly see in this moment that when it comes to instruction and assessment, Mr. Allen is working on his own. Just as a guitar is typically a solo instrument, he is the lone source of instruction and feedback in the classroom. This responsibility is all on him, all of the time, with no help from anyone else. If he is not personally strumming his guitar, there is no live music. He is a soloist and the headliner featured in every act. If he is not personally driving activity in the class, there is no opportunity for learning and feedback.

Sometimes the children's voices get loud when he is working with an individual student. One day, as the students are selecting centers, Mr. Allen makes an announcement: "I want to give a reminder that the only people who can hear you are the ones near you. Because Noelle has to do a lot of thinking."

"I forgot," Diamond says in response.

I imagine it is easy to forget to be quiet during centers. Outside of the test days, I do not observe this to be a time that is typically quiet. As he sits with students at the back table to do the ELL assessment, he asks the child being assessed to do a variety of tasks. Pick up and move cards, point at various pictures, identify different sounds. As they move through the test, Mr. Allen speaks in a soft and gentle voice, alternating between reading the assessment guide, shifting test materials around the table, and jotting notes on the assessment sheet. On one of these days, he works with Alyse, a soft-spoken girl with a heart-shaped face and a small chin. Her straight black hair swoops down the right side of her face and back into a thin, wispy ponytail that springs from the back of her head. He presents a picture card with a drawing of a school classroom on it and asks Alyse, "Can you point to the teacher?" She points silently. "What's this? What's this? What's this?" With each repetition, she points to various places on the card. "Very nice." Later he asks, "Write the '*kuh*' sound in the box." Her small hand grasps a yellow, fat pencil, and she writes her responses as he calmly asks her questions. As I sit at a distance from them, his voice sounds muted and easily blends a bit into the noise of the room.

Finally, after fifteen minutes, they have finished this last section of the assessment. Mr. Allen looks at Alyse and exclaims, "Done! You can go back to your center." She steps away from the table, he writes on his paper for a while, readjusts the assessments, and moves on to the next student, beckoning her from her chosen center-based activity. "Lily—you don't need to take out your name, but I need you here." He starts again, administering the final section to Lily. On this particular day, he spends an hour and fifteen minutes out of the six-hour day—all of the morning and afternoon centers times—administering just a few segments of the tests individually to three students. This is a major time commitment in his school day.

As much as Alyse, Lily, and other students might enjoy the one-on-one time with Mr. Allen, these assessment administrations are decidedly not instructional. Although Mr. Allen mentions that "some teachers get subs during testing," he notes that he never does. As a result, the testing supplants individual instruction time. During my time in the class, I notice that on the days when he does not have assessments, Mr. Allen is usually able to do Writer's Workshop, his small-group interventions, and math centers rotations. When it comes to administering the tests, which I observe on nearly 25 percent of the days I visit his class, Mr. Allen's individualized instruction time during centers is scaled way back, much to his chagrin, so that he can complete tests with all twenty-three students within the timeframe given to him by the district. In lieu of Writer's Workshop, the children are given additional unstructured time: "We are going to have a centers part 2 today because I still have to do that test for a little bit longer." At one point, as he is about to start the ELL assessment with the last student, he looks over at me and says, "One more . . ." I immediately feel a sense of relief; he is almost done! Then he adds to his declaration, ". . . 'til next month." He explains to me that, although he is finishing this test, there are more on the horizon, just about all of which have to be administered individually with each student in a quiet setting and are not helpful to his instruction of the students. I sigh, thinking of the disruptions that more tests will bring to their learning. Less time on individual instruction. More student energy focused on doing tasks for which they will not get feedback. I feel discouraged by this prospect.

It is within this context that Mr. Allen engages in the interactions that come with daily instruction. He teaches in a school environment that is supportive in many ways but also is marked by constrained resources, pressure to meet benchmarks, and requirements to devote a great deal of time to completing standardized assessments. In the face of these factors, Mr. Allen works hard to create a space in which his students are given clear expectations for their academic and social learning, and in which he can leverage their mistakes to improve their performance.

PRACTICING THE MISTAKES AWAY: HELPING STUDENTS REFINE ACADEMIC PERFORMANCE

While the children often make mistakes in Mr. Allen's class, he devotes a great deal of attention to what they *can* do correctly. In his interactions with students, Mr. Allen frequently conveys that being right is a positive thing, and something to be proud of. One of his favorite affirmations when students get things right is to tell them, "Kiss your brain." This phrase is often accompanied by a kiss to the palm of his hand and a quick, open-palm pat on the top of his head, a motion that is frequently mimicked by the children. "I think a lot of times I just use 'Kiss your brain' if I'm surprised by something that they knew that I didn't think that they understood, or if they made some higher-level thinking connection to something." Although he can't remember where he first heard of the phrase, it is prevalent in his class. He peppers this simple compliment throughout the day, and it represents one of the many ways that Mr. Allen responds with wonder and excitement when students do something brilliant. "It's like 'Kiss that brain! That was such a great idea you just had.'" Because he only offers this when students get the right answer, by default it emphasizes that producing correct answers is important. At the same time, he is also telling them, in a sense, that he is proud of what they've just done and that they should celebrate themselves, too. I imagine it could potentially motivate the children to give more thoughtful responses, and to seize opportunities to show off advanced knowledge and understanding in order to get this coveted expression of praise.

Often in class, concepts and skills arise that are very tough or "tricky," but they are either within the scope of the kindergarten curriculum or a challenge that a particular child struggles with on a repeated basis. As in music performance, the key to mastering difficult pieces is to push through in practice and keep trying the hard parts until playing the correct notes comes more easily and frequently. Similarly, I observe that when the children are working in a large group, Mr. Allen often uses open inquiry to draw them out, encouraging them to put forth their best guesses to answer his questions. He graciously works through whatever answers they offer, whether they sound right on the first go-around or not.

One morning during their meeting, Mr. Allen is talking to the students in the whole group about sight words, offering an opportunity to think about common words they read and see in class. "So, I've been noticing in your writing—in Writer's Workshop—there are some words that you guys are often trying to write quite a lot. Okay, so what I'm gonna do is, I wrote those words down, and I put a magnet on the back, and I'm going to put them up on the word wall over where all our names are." Looking up at the word wall, I can see a similarly fashioned magnet with each student's name, listed under a large printout that corresponds with the first letter of each name. "So, if you're thinking 'Oooooh, how do I spell that word?,' what can you do?"

"Look up there," several children say, pointing up to the wall.

Mr. Allen mirrors them—reaching his arm up, holding it out toward the word wall. "Look at it right there, and it will be there."

Mr. Allen finds his first card and holds it flat against his chest, hiding the front side from the view of the students. "Who thinks—if you can raise your hand—who knows what word this is?" He flips the card around and shows it to the class.

"*I*!" the children call out in chorus.

Mr. Allen turns the card around and back to his chest, then holds it up again. "Oh, do not call out." He turns his attention to one student. "What do you see?" He lets the student read the letter. Even as others are calling out, he does not acknowledge their answers and maintains focus on the student he called on. "*I*!" Mr. Allen exclaims. "Do you know you just read a word? *I* is a letter that's a word."

They continue on with another "easy-peasy" word: *a*. After the class guesses the word correctly, he gives a couple of students a chance to try it out in a sentence. "I saw *uh* train." "I was *uh* dog." He moves on by drawing another card and, after a quick glance, pushes it against his chest to hide it as well. "This is probably the word that I see kids trying to write the most." He shakes his head left and right as he issues a plea: "Please don't call out. . . . Please don't call out." When he flips the card over toward the class, there is absolute silence in the room.

After a few seconds, one of the children breaks the silence. "*Wars*," he says, lingering a bit on the *r* sound.

"Ooh—close!" After a second, he notices a raised hand and says, "Lily, what do you think? Do you have an idea?" Rather than requesting that someone give him a right answer, he offers Lily a chance to take a guess.

When he calls on her, her raised hand drops to the corner of her mouth. She stares at the card. Out of the silence, one student starts to repeatedly call out guesses. In response, Mr. Allen shakes his head left and right. While looking straight at the kid calling out, he says to the class, "If you're calling out, you will not get a turn to try." He turns his attention back to Lily. "What do you think it is?"

Ten seconds of think time have passed since she was called. Lily looks up at him and admits, "I don't know."

"That's okay," he assures her. He turns to other hands that have been raised. "What do you think, Noelle?"

Noelle drops her hand and tries out the word. "*Worss*," she utters softly, looking up at Mr. Allen. It sounds like it rhymes with the word *norse*.

"Close. It starts with that '*wuh*' sound. Scott."

Like Noelle, Scott says his guess fast. It is quick and quiet. "*Wass*." The way he says it rhymes with the word *mass*.

"It looks like it should be *wass*, doesn't it? And that's why I'm showing you this word." Mr. Allen pauses. To this point, he has gotten four different student responses. *Wars*, *worss*, *wass*, and "I don't know." With each child's attempt, he has affirmed the response given and reassured that it's okay not to know it. "The word isn't *wass*. It's *was*." He repeats it. "*Was*."

Some of the children call out, "That's what I was going to say."

"Good. Kiss your brain," he replies, affirming their self-proclaimed correctness. "If I was going to write it how it sounded, I would write *W-U-Z*, but some words are not written the way that they should be. So, if you're trying to write 'I was,' just look at the word wall. They'll be up there."

As he talks, he holds the "*I*" card and the "*was*" card next to each other in the proper order. "I *was* . . . dancing." Extending his modeling, he makes one more sentence that starts with the words on the three cards, holding them up as he says them. "I . . . *was* . . . a . . . kindergartener when I was five." Mr. Allen demonstrates the new sight word in a sentence in order to place their understanding of the word "in context" and help model the "difference between letters, words, and sentences"—an understanding that he thinks is all too often taken for granted.

Although none of the students sound out the word correctly, Mr. Allen later tells me that he appreciates the attempts that they made, saying that he feels that "the effort is cool." He is glad that Noelle figures out that it started with the sound of *w*, and he gives her credit for this in their interaction. He is very glad that, although she wasn't able to think of an answer, Lily "still felt motivated to raise her hand and take a stab at it and think about it." His response is to "validate it" because he feels "it's not a big deal if she doesn't know—we'll get there." He shares that his favorite mistake in the lesson is actually Scott's, because it applies "everything that I have taught them about letter sounds so far. Yes—*W* says '*wuh*,' *A* says '*ah*,' and *S* says '*ssss*.'" But the focus of the lesson is presenting a few of the exceptions that they "have to know by just learning them," so they can access them quickly in reading and writing.

Even though all of the guesses are wrong, Mr. Allen holds out for a long while before telling students the correct pronunciation for the sight word, allowing them to really think for themselves and sit with it. Like rehearsal for music performance, this is an important task, allowing the students enough time to practice the sight-word skills they are in the process of building. Collecting many answers from around the room is a form of student inquiry during his instruction that allows different students to engage in the process and expresses that he is flexible and open to accepting a wide range of ideas from them. In this case, they are just learning this new word, and they do not come up with the answer for themselves. Later on, when they again go through all of the cards to practice, they still miss it. When this happens, Mr. Allen simply raises his right hand to his cheek, making the class's hand signal for the sound of *W*. "*Was*. It doesn't make sense," he says, shrugging his shoulders.

For sight words, Mr. Allen does explicit teaching, mitigating the blow of wrong answers by explaining the challenges of remembering them. At other times, Mr. Allen arms them in advance with practical tools and strategies, like turning to the word wall to find a sight word, or singing a phrase from the Carole King song "Alligators All Around" to remember a letter sound. The song goes through a different phrase that is helpful to remember the sound of each letter. The first lines start with "*A-alligators all around; B-bursting balloons; C-catching colds; D-doing dishes.*" If they continue to be stuck, he will model the strategy in a way that helps the students find their own way toward the right answer. In Mr. Allen's class, this principle is most readily demonstrated in his small group work with the alphabet sound practice activity of the ABC Bingo game and with Writer's Workshop.

For instance, on almost every day that I visit Mr. Allen's class, I observe him calling over a small group of three girls—Lily, Olivia, and Clara—to play a simple game of ABC Bingo. Seven or eight years earlier, Mr. Allen's mother found the game set at a discount store and donated it to his class. Over the years, he and his students have used it daily, to the point that the bingo cards and accompanying pieces are, as Mr. Allen puts it, "a little loved with time" and "falling apart." Near the start of centers time, as the other children build with blocks, pretend to cook and play house in the dramatic play area, or engage in other self-selected activities, he prepares the table for their daily practice. He grabs a small, plastic basket from the ABC games shelf near his desk and walks across the room toward the short, round worktable positioned near the large floor-to-ceiling window. As he sits down, his body compacts into the small, child-sized chair—the perfect proportion for five- and six-year-olds but a tight fit for a man of average height. Yet, I watch him ease into the tiny chair, expertly folding his legs to the side comfortably. When everything is set up, he calls the students over to work with him.

"I need my girls who I play ABC Bingo with." The students are identified for intervention based on Mr. Allen's frequent informal testing, and he tracks information about their knowledge of uppercase and lower-case letter recognition—as well as letter-sound recognition—in his private Google doc. Looking to expand support for Reader's Workshop, he started integrating this game into his class years ago as a "literacy activity that kids could engage in that wasn't necessarily a guided reading book for kids who aren't necessarily reading yet." In the fall of each school year, he uses the game with students who need help building letter-shape recognition—focusing first on uppercase letters and then, once that is better known, moving on to lowercase. Now, as they are in the second half of the school year, he focuses on letter-sound recognition. At the moment he works with these three girls, but the membership of this small intervention group has shifted over the course of the year as student abilities progress. Early in my time visiting his class, I gladly watch as one girl learns enough of the letter-sound matches that he no longer requires her to do the daily intervention.

One by one, Clara, Lily, and Olivia come from different centers around the room and find a chair at the small table. They have played this game many times and know what to do. Once there, they begin to look through the set of bingo cards in the pile.

"All right," says Mr. Allen. "Pick quick because once you decide, you can't change it." With this reminder, each girl makes her final selection, drawing it close and settling into her seat to wait for the game to start.

At the center of the table, within an arm's reach of all three students, sits the white, rectangular basket. In it are several laminated bingo cards and markers, worn and slightly curled from many years of daily use, featuring the image of a smiling cartoon puppy with white fur and large, tan spots encircling his eyes. The girls are sitting still and quiet, calmly waiting for the game to begin. Mr. Allen removes a baggie from the game box and draws a card from it, launching the game without further instruction. "Okay. Ready. If you have one of the letters—or both of the letters—that make the '*kuh*' sound."

The three girls drop their gaze to look down at their boards. With the letter sound in mind, their eyes search their small bingo boards, scanning the grapheme pair options contained within each square of their four-by-two playing cards—eight possibilities in total. With each letter drawn from the baggie, they either reach out toward the basket to grab one of the well-worn bingo markers—decorated with the smiling puppy's face—or quietly wait for the next sound to be called. In this case, Lily reaches out for a marker to put on the *Cc*.

"Which one is it, Lily?" She silently picks up the marker and draws it toward a spot on her board.

Mr. Allen's eyes track Lily's hand as she places the marker. In a flat, matter-of-fact voice he says, "*C* makes the '*kuh*' sound."

At some points, the girls silently play the game, and Mr. Allen calls one sound after another without interruption. But there are always a few letters that trip up the girls—either by mixing up the sounds or by error of omission. In one particular session, he calls out the letter *Y*, and they have some trouble remembering the matching letter sound.

"If you have the letter that makes the '*yuh*' sound . . ."

Clara looks up at him with a broad smile and asks, "*U*?"

"Not *U*," he says. "It should be *U*, but it's not." In this moment, Mr. Allen both affirms Clara's guess, while also clearly indicating that she is not correct. Clara continues to smile as she drops her head down toward her game board.

Olivia chimes in, "*W*?"

"It sounds like it could be *W*, too," he says, again affirming the response. "*Y. Yuh*—yo-yo. *Yakkity-yak*." As he gives the right answer, it is accompanied by a swift reminder of ways they can use the tools and strategies he's given them to remember the sound in the future—"*yuh*" as the sound of *Y*; yo-yo—the image for the letter *Y* from their Writer's Workshop ABC chart; and "*yakkity-yak*" from the "Alligators All Around" song. Mr. Allen pauses as they correct their boards. Olivia grabs a marker from the basket and places it on her game board.

"So, what sound does *y* make, everybody?" The girls are very quiet. "*Yuh*. Say it with me." He chants, again repeating the sound—"*Y* says *yuh. Y* says *yuh.*" Clara and Lily softly mumble the chant with him, and Olivia lets out a loud burst of the letter sound. "*Yuh!*" she sings, lifting her body slightly out of her chair as she holds the note.

In the middle of this recitation, Olivia folds her right hand into a thumbs-up and begins moving it slowing up toward the ceiling. In this motion, she is making a nonverbal symbol for the letter *U*, a hand motion that Mr. Allen adopted from a curriculum in order to help students remember the easily confused sounds of the different short vowels. With wide eyes and a smile, Mr. Allen reaches out toward Olivia and softly taps her hand, gently pushing it back toward the table. "That's *U* for *uh*." Olivia slinks back into the chair and matches his smile, her hands dropping to her lap as the big curls of her long, brown hair fall over the back of the chair. "Close, though!" he says, tapping her gently on the shoulder with his pointer finger. "You're knowing those—you're very close. English is a silly language with weird sounds."

"It's like crazy. Crazy," says Olivia.

"It's Crazytown," he agrees. "Population: Us."

In this instance, Mr. Allen gently corrects the students as they make mistakes, offering them opportunities to guess. In general, when the girls make mistakes during ABC Bingo, Mr. Allen softens the blow, but he does make sure they eventually land on the right answer. When they cannot find the answers on their own, he offers gentle reminders of previously taught strategies they can use to help them out in the future. And, as he commonly does in the classroom, he winds it down with a little joke. In this case, it is one that helps the students understand why this might be so hard for them—the English language has weird sounds. Although the students do respond to the feedback about their mistakes with subtle changes in body language, the girls remain smiling and engaged with their teacher throughout the activity. In the interaction, I observe that Mr. Allen strikes a balance between giving the children think time to ponder the letter-sound matches, and giving them the answers for the items they do not yet know how to identify.

In his work to help the students become independent and self-reflective learners, Mr. Allen balances many considerations in order to put his principles into practice. When students make mistakes, or have a hard time figuring out an answer, he toggles between offering hints, asking questions, and providing mini lessons to help them find their way to the right answers for themselves. As illustrated in these examples during

ABC Bingo, he engages in a process in which he gives the students time to try to figure it out. When children make mistakes, he tries to "bring it to their attention and see if they can catch it without me having to tell them what it is. . . . [I try to] let them look at it and think about it for a little bit, and then maybe my hint will get a little more specific if they're not quite getting it right away." A key part of his philosophy of teaching is about helping the students help themselves. He "would much rather . . . teach them how to edit and be reflective of their own work, rather than me just fixing it for them because then they won't get any skills . . . or tools of their own when it comes to doing it later." I observe, time and again, that when students struggle, Mr. Allen frames their mistakes as challenges, and reminds them of the knowledge and capabilities they already have to fix the problem for themselves.

As the year marches forward, he shifts the focus of the small group from rote identifications to familiarity with books. While these foundational skills are important, he is also concerned with other elements of reading, and exchanges the ABC Bingo game for time with simple readers that emphasize "more print concepts, more reading behaviors like turning the page, there's a word on the page they can point to." In addition to teaching them to recognize letter shapes and sounds, Mr. Allen also wants "them to be able to have a book" because "they start to notice what their peers are able to do and what they're not." Some of the girls in the ABC Bingo group continue to need "consistent help" through the rest of the year. Going into first grade, he recommends some for a Reading Recovery intervention to help them continue to face these mistakes head on and build their reading abilities. With these daily efforts, he offers continued opportunities to increase correct letter-sound identifications, setting them up as best he can for the challenges that lie ahead in the next grades.

One of the times that the children can put these skills to use is during Writer's Workshop. During this time, Mr. Allen assembles the students in small groups and offers individualized feedback as they independently develop stories, write details, and produce illustrations.

> Writer's Workshop is probably my favorite thing to teach because it gives you a real snapshot of what they are able to do in that moment. You can look at their work, you can talk to them about their work, and you can see what the next steps are a little more clearly. Like, oh, this kid is having a hard time coming up with a story. . . . This kid's having

difficulty drawing people. This kid's having difficulty putting a space between words.

In this time, he can pinpoint areas for skill development and offer an open forum to "go practice" what is learned in more structured activities, like ABC Bingo.

During Writer's Workshop, the students sit at a round table, each with their own folder, paper, and pencil. On one particular Wednesday, Mr. Allen is working with one of five small groups at the round table next to the window—the same place where he plays ABC Bingo. He carefully tracks each student's story topic in a computer document, and in this group, they have self-selected a wide array of topics. On this day, Taj is writing about a trip to the aquarium; Stella is writing about riding her bicycle; and Olivia is writing a story about the time she spent with her friend, Abigail. From his seat, Mr. Allen shifts his attention to each of the students at the table, skillfully engaging them individually, and rapidly shifting his focus from one to another, as needed. It almost looks like a type of juggling—he keeps each student moving in their own path, all at the same time, offering just-in-time feedback so they can continually, and individually, move their work ahead. During the workshop, each student is typically at a different point in the writing process. Some are developing new ideas, while others are illustrating and adding story details; and then they use invented spelling to independently write the story text. Mr. Allen feels that because "it's a workshop, the point is to look at it and see the things that are going really well, and then kind of offer suggestions for what they can try next time." He also appreciates that, unlike worksheets that are more prescribed and finite, "Writer's Workshop is never really done. We can leave things be or we can come back to them, or we can decide we're not gonna work on them anymore. But it's a process. There's no real end." To Mr. Allen, this is an exciting opportunity for learning in his classroom.

At one point, while discussing her story with Mr. Allen, Olivia shares her current sentence. "ALL day I played with my friend Abigail." Olivia starts in on writing out her sentence. "Ahhhhhhhhhh-ll day"—her eyes are wide, mouth open in a round *O* shape.

Mr. Allen pauses Olivia's writing with a simple question: "What was the best thing that you did?"

Olivia stops writing and thinks for a moment "Uuuum. Whole thing."

"Well," he says. "Pick one thing that you can draw a picture of."

"I can draw everything!" says Olivia, excitedly.

"I want you to start with one and if we need another page, we can add another." With this request, Mr. Allen redirects Olivia and offers additional focus to the task that can help her to sidestep potential ambiguity, confusion, and frustration later on when trying to figure out how to illustrate her experience. "So, what was the first thing you played?" he asks, eliciting specific details from her real-life experience.

"Uh, we played. While we were at the science museum."

"So, okay, what were you doing at the science museum?" he inquires. Mr. Allen continues to go back and forth with Olivia. Through specific question-asking, his tone of voice, and his long-held attention, he expresses interest in learning more about her experience, without dampening her enthusiasm for her story. The result is that he helps her to focus in enough so that the story-writing task is broken down into more manageable chunks, a strategy she can successfully implement on her own later. With several volleys back and forth, Mr. Allen helps Olivia to select and describe one of the many, specific events she experienced with her friend. "So, start drawing you and your friend on that climbing structure," he suggests, turning his attention back to other students as Olivia gets to work with her detailed illustration.

Although less concrete than counting correctly or identifying facts from a story, the mistakes I observe in Writer's Workshop are more about rushing through a process or omitting details. With Mr. Allen's approach—focused on helping students to think things out—he promotes Olivia's growth in both her current and future writing. Without this interaction, it is possible that Olivia may have gone in many different directions with her story, perhaps not focusing enough to write a single story event that could be captured on one page. Mr. Allen asks questions to draw out richer, more detailed work from Olivia and the other students. In his view, "the motivation and the learning come from the questions, and I have a more authentic picture of what they know and understand by asking them a question rather than giving them answers all day." With this interaction, he provides an opportunity for Olivia to practice refining and articulating story details in a process that he is scaffolding but she is driving.

Some students are very excited about their stories and, like Olivia, they have lots of details that they want to include. Other students are eager to complete the task, and they rush to finish. In these latter instances, particularly when it comes to writing, Mr. Allen intervenes, prompting students to slow down. For instance, on another day during Writer's Workshop, Mr. Allen and his students from a different small group huddle at the round table near the back of the room. He slowly shifts his attention from one paper to another, pausing for feedback along the way. At one point, he tells Ahmed, "I want you to slow down so your letters are perfect, so I can really read it," pushing for him to make his best effort in penmanship. Then, as he makes his way around the table, his eyes are drawn to the paper in front of Angelo, a small Asian boy with dark brown eyes, brown hair, and a slight lisp. At that moment, he is drawing a picture of himself and his brother riding the subway train—both with their whole bodies colored bright yellow, and without clothing. As Mr. Allen's gaze drifts to Angelo's paper, his eyebrows rise. "In Writer's Workshop, there's no rushing," he says. "I want you to do your *best* best job." When later reflecting on this interaction, Mr. Allen shares with me that, by repeating the word, he is emphasizing to Angelo that, with benchmarks like his stack of monthly self-portraits from over the year, he knows what Angelo's "*best* best looks like. This isn't it. What can we do to make it more like that?" Mr. Allen can sense the resistance that Angelo has to the activity. Although he technically is completing his work, his mistake is that he has rushed and, by comparison to Angelo's prior drawings and writing, is not giving the task his all.

After Mr. Allen's comment about rushing, Angelo sits quietly in his chair for a few moments. He turns and looks at his neighbor's paper and asks about the lasers she is drawing. His pencil twirls in his right hand. And after some time has passed, without making any revisions, he holds his paper up toward Mr. Allen, tucking the top edge of it into his mouth, between his lips.

Looking at the unaltered drawing, Mr. Allen urges Angelo to improve his work. "I want you to add more details about you and your brother. You look like mustard." With this response, he is playfully "trying to joke with him a little bit" in order to motivate him to put in more effort to make his illustration better represent what he looks like in real life.

With the paper still in the air, Angelo retorts, "Is it because I ate so much mustard and I turned into mustard?"

"Nice try, Angelo," says Mr. Allen. "I want you to pick out an outfit for you and your brother." This is a type of prompt I have observed many times during Mr. Allen's Writer's Workshop. Again and again, he reminds students to carefully attend to and represent the fine-grained details of their experiences.

Angelo works for about two more seconds, then holds it up again, tapping it to get Mr. Allen's attention. "Am I done?"

"What do you think?" asks Mr. Allen. "What more details could you add?"

Angelo looks at his paper. "Houses." Mr. Allen returns his attention to other students and Angelo gets to work drawing some big squares on his paper, surrounding his sketch of his brother and himself. Twenty seconds pass, and he is already checking in again with Mr. Allen about the picture.

"Okay, which one is you and which one is Frankie? I think you have brown hair."

In response, Angelo grabs the brown crayon and swirls the brown around the page in a circular motion for a few seconds, then holds the paper up again toward his teacher. Mr. Allen looks at his work again. "What about labeling you and your brother and the subway train?" He turns back to another student, prompting details from her, too.

Before the teacher can turn around, Angelo holds his paper up again. With furrowed eyebrows, Mr. Allen looks at Angelo for a few moments before again asking, "Where are your labels?" Angelo continues to resist and the conversation shifts—he indicates that he does not want to keep doing this. "Well, that's Writer's Workshop. At school, sometimes you do things that aren't your favorite. 'Cause when I show this to your mom, I want her to say, 'Wow, Angelo really did his best.' Not 'Wow, I think Angelo rushed.'"

Angelo resists throughout the session. As the time in Writer's Workshop draws to a close, Mr. Allen makes a general announcement to the table for the benefit of Angelo and the other students. "I'm gonna let you guys be done, but next time I want to see a lot less rushing. . . . I know what your best work looks like. This is your rushing work."

Later reflecting on this teaching moment, Mr. Allen tells me,

> If Angelo was unable to do those things—if he couldn't differentiate between colors, if he couldn't draw details about setting, if he couldn't hear sounds and write them down—I wouldn't have pushed it so much. But he was capable of doing all of those things—he just didn't feel like it. . . . Sometimes in school there are things that are have-tos.

Because he knows what Angelo is capable of and has evidence of how much he has grown over the year, Mr. Allen continues to push him, despite his resistance. In that context, he considers not trying your hardest to be a mistake, as trying your best is an expectation of the class. Because Mr. Allen has the students draw a monthly self-portrait—which are clipped on a bulletin board in his classroom—he has a good sense of Angelo's drawing and writing abilities and can tell he is not performing at his best. "Thank goodness for those self-portraits. I think they epitomize what their absolute best drawing is, so it's something that I can point to." This strategy allows him to not only have concrete information about the students' capabilities but also to have leverage to push them when they aren't giving their all in their work. Having a tangible reference to point to helps Mr. Allen hold the students accountable to him and to themselves.

TUNING THE STRINGS: REFINING STUDENTS' CLASSROOM BEHAVIOR

Although teaching often revolves around academic skills and content, much of the work of an early childhood educator involves the social development of children. Additionally, to get things done with academics, behavior management is necessarily a central aspect of the workings of the classroom and the interactions around mistakes. Accordingly, Mr. Allen works not only to help the students to practice their kindergarten academic performance but for them to learn and fine-tune the social skills that will allow them to operate effectively in school, both in his class and beyond.

Mr. Allen's classroom has clear rules and expectations about how the kindergarteners should operate in the room, how they should move their bodies around the shared spaces, how they should engage in their work, and how they should treat each other. When students do not meet these norms, they receive corrective feedback from Mr. Allen, indicating that they need to adjust their actions. In this sense, misbehavior is a type of mistake, particularly when one of Mr. Allen's central goals is to help them become better citizens and learn how to operate in a classroom, so that they will be ready for upper grades. He "rolls out" his expectations "slowly" in the beginning of the year because he feels that if he introduces "too many things, all at once, none of it is really gonna get done." He particularly focuses on reinforcing three main facets of their behavior: kindness, working hard, and trustworthiness. He remarks, "Those are words we hear an awful lot in Mr. Allen's class." He spends a great deal of time "hammering in" the meaning of these words and helping to build a "stockpile of moments" from their experience in the class to give the concepts meaning.

Reflecting on his teaching, Mr. Allen tells me, "I feel like I'm very clear about behaviors and what they should look and sound like at different times. And there are some kids that just need to be redirected a lot." In his kindergarten classroom, Mr. Allen offers as much—if not more— corrective feedback on student behaviors and social choices as on their academic work. As demonstrated earlier, his correction of academic mistakes tends to be focused on helping students correct themselves and are shared in a gentle way. When classroom rules are broken or social norms are breached, he continues to try to promote self-regulation, but he is much sterner in his tone and approach when communicating about these mistakes with the children.

For instance, a phrase I commonly hear from Mr. Allen is "I'm worried." When Mr. Allen starts to worry, it is a signal to his class that their behavior is not meeting his expectations. He uses the phrase on an almost daily basis, as the students test boundaries of the rules and lose focus at various points in the day. Rather than tell them directly the choice that he wants them to make, the phrase "I'm worried" signals that it is time for them to reassess what they're doing and think about what is expected of them.

Each day at the start of centers time, Mr. Allen passes out what he calls "names"—printed photographs of each child with a label affixed to it displaying the person's first name. The centers chart hangs near the floor on a closed storage closet door in the room. It has several rows of long, narrow, clear plastic pockets, and on the left side is a column of choices the children can select. Mr. Allen calls the students' names one by one, at which time they are individually dismissed from the meeting area and can go over to wait in line for a turn to place their name cards next to the center where they wish to play. The order matters, and as the children line up to make their choices, Mr. Allen is worried about the volume of noise in the classroom. "I'm gonna remind you—thank you, Olivia—you're being a great listener," he says, pointing at Olivia. "Amelia—you are being a great listener—your eyes are on me. Thank you, Diamond." Mr. Allen reaches down to a child just in front of him, places a hand gently on his shoulder and, looking him in his eyes, asks, "Are you with me, too? Are you with me right now?" The boy shakes his head up and down in response to Mr. Allen's softly spoken questions. "Thank you."

Mr. Allen broadens his attention back to the whole class. "I need quiet, calm voices and quiet, calm bodies today." He pauses for a moment, looking at the students. As he continues, I watch tension enter his face, as the skin on his forehead starts to form thick wrinkles. "Okay? I had to tell people a lot of reminders yesterday. To the point where they had to leave the centers they were in because I had to remind them so many times. And I said, 'If I have to remind you about how loud you're being one more time, you're going to have to leave and go to a different center.'" He shakes his pointer finger at the class as he reenacts what he told them on the prior day. "Did I really do that?"

"Yeah," reply a few students in unison.

"I did," he affirms. "Do I like doing that?"

"No!" the class yells.

"Absolutely not. I want you to be able to play in the center that you want to play in. But if you're going to be loud and rude to your friends, Kevin, who are trying to take the test, you will not be able to be at the center you want to be at." He shakes his head left and right a few times, indicating their choices will be restricted. "Okay? Who's going to do a great job using quiet, calm voices?" Before he can even finish the question, the students raise their hands into the air, giving him an affirmative thumbs-up sign. He mirrors their gesture as he pivots his head slowly, looking at the quiet thumbs-up across the room. "Awesome!" he says with a nod. "Thank you." He continues to pass out the name cards and the children carry on, quietly making their selections for centers.

The mistake in this moment is that students are not paying attention during the group meeting and transition to centers, and Mr. Allen does several things to help them self-correct their behavior. First, he pauses the action of the classroom and, by professing his state of worry, he makes them aware that something is not as it should be. Then, in addition to clearly describing the behavior he wants from them, he also draws attention to students who are already meeting the expectations. In doing so, it affirms those students, and it encourages other students who are not on task to turn to their peers to see nearby models of expected behavior that they can copy themselves. Next, he uses a series of questions to help the children recall past events, reminding them of the consequences for not shifting their behavior. And finally, he asks for a pledge from them, that they will continue to use "quiet, calm voices," thanking them in advance for their adherence to the norms. Moments like this are helpful to recenter the children in the immediate moment and to get the class back on task, as well as a means to help prevent these sorts of misbehaviors in the future.

Another way Mr. Allen helps students understand the expected norms of politeness is through Emily Post, an early twentieth-century author who published books on manners, including her best-selling book *Etiquette in Society, in Business, in Politics, and at Home*. Mr. Allen was first introduced to Emily Post as a college senior during a brunch focused on teaching etiquette. At this event, the presenter emphasized the importance of knowing the "norms of eating" that would be useful when "entering the business world" and having meetings in fancy restaurants with "a potential client or a future boss." Although Mr. Allen does not feel like he is a part of that particular social world, he "loves the fanfare of it all" and has carried these lessons on etiquette forward. He began referencing Emily Post in his classroom just a few years back, and she has become a central figure in the class ever since, particularly in relation to eating, and how students interact with others following norms of politeness. Each year, he shares a children's book with them called *Emily's Everyday Manners*, along with another book called *Do Unto Otters*. These stories both center on manners, and the books—as well as the embodiment of the ideals of Emily Post—become a reference point for the year.

From *Emily's Everyday Manners*:

> Emily and Ethan love their family and friends. They want them to feel good. So, they do kind things for others and use manners every day.
>
> Good manners take practice. Sometimes family and you can forget. But they never give up trying!

This storybook and the legendary status of Emily Post serve as both models and aspirations for how the children should strive to behave and treat each other in their classroom community. Mr. Allen enacts the principles through both positive comments about student behavior—"It is nice to have a calm, Emily Post snack with our friends"—and through corrective feedback dissuading rude student behavior—"Push your body all the way [in to the table]. Emily Post!"

I find it interesting to witness just how powerful the influence of Emily Post is in this class. I see on multiple occasions that the students do correct inconsiderate behavior when they are simply reminded of her name. For example, one day during centers time, several children are playing in the block area, and the expansive structure they were building extends over into the neighboring dramatic play area. Ahmed quietly slips away from the block area and tries to shift to a different section of the room, sidestepping the big task of clean up.

Mr. Allen sees this and calls him over for a heart-to-heart talk. "You were just allowed to return to the area yesterday." He continues to talk through this individually with Ahmed, drawing his attention to the blocks, which cover the floor and are thickly stacked on top of each other. After they finish their discussion, Ahmed and the other boys start to work together to pick up the pieces. Mr. Allen continues to chat with them about the border for the area, asking them where the edge is between blocks and dramatic play.

After talking with them about this for a little while, he walks over to the piano, picks up the picture of Emily Post, places it on a shelf facing them in the block area, and simply asks "What would she think?" As Mr. Allen walks away and turns his attention to other activities in the room, the group of boys in the block area, including Ahmed, continue working diligently to put away the blocks on their own. After observing that the boys were having a lot of trouble cleaning up, I am surprised to see that just a few minutes after the picture was brought over, the area is completely cleaned up and they each have moved on to another center. This is an example of the way that the physical object of the framed photo can serve as a "nice little visual reminder" of polite and responsible classroom behavior, and an easy way for Mr. Allen to remind them of the right thing to do, just by saying, "She's watching you from afar!"

While sometimes Mr. Allen has a direct Emily Post intervention, as in the case of the sprawling block area, she is just a simple reference at other times. Almost daily, either Mr. Allen or his aide, Mrs. Stanton, reference Emily Post during snack time. When the students are being loud, talking with food in their mouths, or don't wait for all of their friends to get their snacks before they start eating, he draws attention to it. "There are a few people I would not want to take to a fancy restaurant." When the children are demonstrating nice manners, he also brings it to their attention. On occasion, they eat quietly as soft music plays in the background:

> It is totally okay to talk in a soft voice with the table. You don't need to yell to be heard. The only people who need to hear you are right next to you. Oh, it's so much better in here. . . . If you can hear the harp music, you are doing the right thing. And your friends are doing the right thing. It is nice to have a peaceful snack with our friends where we speak in calm voices and don't yell at each other.

In short, the students' relationship with the larger-than-life Emily Post allows a clear model of expectations that help Mr. Allen to correct impolite behaviors as they arise. He views the framed photograph of Emily to be a means of feedback for the children that he can "just point to" if someone is being rude. He hopes that, both within his class and long after, she can serve as "a great example of remembering manners and remembering to be polite," as well as "group norms of friendliness and turn-taking." Thinking back to my experience as a kindergarten teacher, I can understand just how necessary it can be to make these sorts of abstract ideas more tangible for students. I can also imagine that some people, watching from the sidelines, may have some questions about using the picture of an elderly White woman as a model of behavior for a diverse class of young students. But, as far as I can tell, it is an effective way for Mr. Allen to help the children learn how to be considerate of each other, and reinforces the attributes of trustworthiness and kindness, two highly esteemed values in their classroom community. Emily Post seems like a positive addition to the class, and she helps students to have clear ideas about how to monitor and self-correct their own behaviors. Her picture serves as a simple prompt for students to assess and adjust their actions according to the norms they have learned, with little intervention from Mr. Allen.

In that same vein, Mr. Allen often gives students time for a do-over to correct their group behaviors. When the students collectively lose focus, he squeezes his eyes shut and says, "I need my meeting back in three, two, one, zero." His eyelids lift back open again, he looks out at the class, and continues with the activity.

The countdown to reset is a common classroom management technique that Mr. Allen uses. When students are talking over him when he is speaking, or children are calling out answers rather than raising their hands, he breaks through the noise with a simple countdown. Often this response happens as the children are sitting on the rug, having a discussion as a class, or as they start calling out or yelling out answers.

He quickly counts down relatively often to reset the class if they are talking during the meeting. However, if their attention gets too unfocused, which happens occasionally, he takes it further than simply closing his eyes. For instance, one morning the students are talking loudly as Mr. Allen is preparing to review the daily schedule with them. The volume level in the room gets loud, and some children are not focusing their attention on him and the schedule; instead, they are debating about whether or not the word *crazy* is a bad word. Suddenly, his brow furrows, ushering a worried look onto his face. He pauses and says, "You know what? I'm gonna leave and come back, and when I come back, people are going to know not to call out." The room falls silent. As the children look on, Mr. Allen stands up. He begins the short journey from his teacher's chair—stepping around them as they sit on the rug in the meeting area—to the door just behind them at the back of the room. Once there, he reaches his hand into his left pocket, pulling out his keys, looking at them and using them to unlock the door. As he does this, the children continue to watch. A few are smiling and seem to be holding back a laugh, but most are silent with serious faces, tracking his every move. After several seconds, he kicks the doorstop to the side with his foot and raises his hand to give a quick wave to the class as he exits the room. The heavy metal door, which is almost always propped open, closes with a thud. This is a lengthy process, during which time the students' necks are turned behind them, watching every step with blank looks on their faces. After he has left the room, the silence continues. The children begin to break their attention from the door, looking around the room and at each other, momentarily teacherless.

After four seconds in the hallway, Mr. Allen opens the door and reenters the room. "Good morning, everyone," he says in a hushed voice, pushing the door back open and repositioning the doorstop.

"Good morning, Mr. Allen," the children say sweetly in chorus, necks backward to face him as he speaks. Several serious faces blossom into smiles as they quietly continue to watch him.

Mr. Allen addresses the class from the door. "I am going to come to my seat, and I am expecting great school listening looks. That means eyes are watching, ears are listening, voices are quiet, bodies are still, and hand is raised when you'd like to talk." After this reminder of the expected behavior, he walks up to his chair and turns to face the class. Once he arrives, he looks at the students. Stretching his pointer finger toward Noelle, he says, "Noelle, I love your school listening look. Alex, love it." The children all sit quietly, watching Mr. Allen as he talks. He then makes his way around the room saying "Love it. Love it. Love it. Love it. Love it . . ." on and on in a rapid-fire rhythm, making eye contact and pointing to a different child with each repetition of the phrase. When his gaze reaches the last of the students—a boy who is sitting quietly in that moment but often is not focused or quiet during group meetings—he says, "Extra love it. That's 100 percent right there." Then, without missing a beat, he picks up where they left off, reviewing the day's schedule.

After a frenzied moment in which the students collectively lose their focus during the group meeting, Mr. Allen gives them a chance to have a do-over. By leaving the room or, in other instances, by closing his eyes and counting backward down to zero, he signals to the children that they have a chance to gather themselves and refocus outside of his watchful eye. When he gives them that second chance, time and again, they rise to the occasion, recalibrating and offering the "school listening looks" requested by their teacher. Although the interaction begins with a statement of expectations not being met (e.g., telling them they need to not call out), it ends with praise and continuance of their learning—with focus.

STRUMMING THROUGH CYCLES OF LIFE

> Things are going to get messed up and things aren't going to be clean and neat all the time. But if you can look at where they are in September and then where they are in June, you will see a world of growth if you're patient enough to let the process run its course.
> – Mr. Allen

Mr. Allen goes through quite a journey with his students over the course of the year in kindergarten. Working in a context of high pressure to meet district end-of-year benchmarks, Mr. Allen is clear that getting things right is important. But he also creates space for students to think; he allows opportunities to self-correct behaviors and mistakes in academic work; and he protects children's opportunities to hypothesize and try out new ideas. Throughout each day, Mr. Allen demonstrates in his class that he values opportunities for students to learn to do and think for themselves. In addition, when he is working with students who have made mistakes, he feels that if you "just fix them without any explanation, you're denying an opportunity for growth." With the passing of time, each child will grow and move forward, if given the opportunity to try, to make mistakes, and to learn.

Mr. Allen frequently grabs his guitar and sings with his students. As he easily strums the strings on the instrument and sings in his beautiful tenor voice, the children join him in singing while sitting on the rug in the library. As with his teaching, he takes the second-hand guitar into his arms; he applies his expertise and experience with the instrument to sing old songs that he knows and loves, and makes beautiful music with it, just as it is. No matter the state of his instrument or his limited access to classroom resources, Mr. Allen tries hard to create the best music and the *best* best learning that he can for the children in his care.

2

MS. RIVERS

Coaching the Team Toward "Perfect Perfect" Performance

For the morning read-aloud, Alana Rivers sits at the front of her class reading the Eric Carle book *The Tiny Seed*. There is an air of calm in the room as the class prepares to resume their collective learning activities immediately after a brief snack break. Ms. Rivers opens the book and makes her way through the first few pages, with the children peering up from the floor.

As is customary in many kindergarten classrooms, Ms. Rivers's students sit on a brightly colored rug for this teacher-led story reading. The area serves as the heart of this classroom; the children and Ms. Rivers spend the majority of their days here, engaged in practice activities and discussions. The oversized floor rug is comprised of thirty-five distinct squares; a five-by-seven grid forms a rainbow of large, colored stripes— red, orange, yellow, light green, green, blue, and purple. The children sit on their own individual "color spots" in a tight formation, each quiet and still with legs "criss-cross" and eyes squarely focused on Ms. Rivers and the book page. From my perch to the back and side of the group, the students' uniforms look as if they meld together into a sea of collared crimson shirts, distinguished by a wide variety of hair styles and textures. In appearance, Ms. Rivers stands out from her students, as she is a White woman dressed simply and comfortably in a cream-colored, long-sleeved sweater and dark pants. Her long, thick, jet-black hair cascades over her shoulder and down her arm, secured only by a small hair tie to keep it out of her way.

Page by page, *The Tiny Seed* chronicles the fate of seeds that journey to different landscapes (e.g., icy mountain, ocean) as they are dispersed to distant places by the autumn winds. The book dovetails nicely with the class's current science unit on "Living Things" and, with each page, the teacher asks the children questions to help bolster this connection. Soon, Ms. Rivers reads a line that says, "One seed drifts down onto the desert. It is hot and dry and the seed cannot grow." The page shows an illustration of a brown and grey, sandy expanse, punctuated with a cluster of three small cacti. Before continuing to the next line, Ms. Rivers poses a question: "How come the seed can't grow? It's got soil." Several students raise their hands, willing to respond, and she calls on them in turn.

The first student, Mateo, suggests that it is because the soil is hard. Despite a second read through of the line of text, he remains convinced that the author said this explicitly in the story.

"They didn't actually. Why don't I read it again?" Ms. Rivers suggests in a calm voice. "Listen really carefully. It says, 'It is hot and dry.'" Ms. Rivers looks right at Mateo and shakes her head left and right. "Doesn't say the soil is hard. Okay? You did a good job reading the story again and thinking about what's in the story." She points at her forehead, adding, "Now we need to use our brain to figure out why the seed can't grow. So, we need to add onto that a little bit. Can someone add on to what Mateo said and tell us more about why the seed can't grow?"

Again, many hands shoot up into the air.

Ms. Rivers continues: "He said it's because it's dry there, but we need more information. What do you know in your brain?" She pauses and looks around the room before selecting the next respondent. "Track Camilla. Camilla, why can't the seed grow there?"

Camilla sits with a dark, long-sleeved sweater over her uniform shirt today; her black, wavy hair is pulled into a loose ponytail that sprouts from the back of her head and hangs down to her upper back. She rocks slightly in place as she speaks from her color spot in the back row. With the words "Track Camilla," the children sitting in the rows up front shift their attention to intensely watch—or "track"—their classmate, which requires most of them to crane their necks and bodies around 180 degrees. "Because when something's dry, seeds don't have anything they need. Because they need water, soil, and air . . . and air."

"So, Camilla," responds Ms. Rivers, "you're telling us everything that you know a seed needs, but you need to focus on this question." Ms. Rivers points at the pages of the book and looks right at her as she again asks, "Why can't *this* seed grow?" Although Camilla's response does include some correct information about how seeds grow, based on her teacher's feedback, I perceive that the child is close to the answer Ms. Rivers is going for, but she is not quite there. I watch with rapt attention as this exchange continues to unfold and the spotlight remains on Camilla for a while longer. "Track Camilla again," Ms. Rivers says. "I think she's got it."

Camilla continues hesitantly as her fellow kindergarteners sustain their focused gaze on her. "Everything the seed needs . . . the seed has soil . . . and it needs other things so it can grow."

"Like what?" probes Ms. Rivers. "Do you think that seed has air?" She pauses for a moment or two, allowing Camilla to consider this. "It does because air is everywhere," Ms. Rivers explains, waving over the expanse of the two-page book illustration and looking at Camilla with wide eyes. "Just like there's air all around us now. That seed also has air." This direct rebuttal makes very clear that Camilla, like Mateo, has not provided the correct answer that the teacher seeks.

Ms. Rivers briefly pauses and looks around at the other children before she opens the floor for more guesses. "Why don't we ask somebody else? Somebody who can use words to explain."

Hands go up in the air again.

As the next child, Nikki, closely echoes Camilla's previous answer, Ms. Rivers's mouth forms a tight-lipped grin. "Nikki. You're repeating what Camilla said." She shakes her head left and right as she adds, "That doesn't help us learn." Ms. Rivers waves her arm to beckon reengagement from everyone. "Why don't we start again? I'll go back and read, I'll ask the question again, and then we can think about it together."

Ms. Rivers reads the line from the text for the third time and offers an immediate restatement of the information. "The book told us that this seed is in the desert, and that the desert is hot and dry." She pauses for a moment and looks up at the students, gesturing with her right hand as she talks. "We have to use that information and what we know about what seeds need to think about why this seed is not growing. Do you all know what hot means?"

"Yeah," says the group.

"I'm thinking about what I know about what seeds need to grow." Ms. Rivers shakes her head left and right as she shares, "I don't remember anything about the temperature." She pauses and the children sit in a quick second of silence pondering this idea before the teacher continues with her explanation. "Hot or cold—so that's not as important. Do you all know what dry means?"

A few students call out, "Yeah."

"I'm thinking about what I know about what seeds need. If the desert is dry, then there's something that a seed needs that it is not getting. What is that thing?" She emphatically thrusts one pointer finger up in the air as nearly every child's hand rises. "One thing. It has to do with the word *dry*." There are numerous hands to choose from, but she waits another couple of seconds before she calls on the next speaker. "Marisol."

"Water," says Marisol.

"Yep," Ms. Rivers affirms. "Because if something is dry, it means it's not . . ."

Two different students offer the wrong answer to this fill-in-the-blank statement, back to back and in rapid succession. Each time Ms. Rivers smiles and politely but quickly declines their responses, explains why they are wrong, repeats the prompt, and moves on. Within fifteen seconds, she gets to the third hand. "Tiana—something dry is not . . ."

"Is not wet?" Tiana states tentatively.

"Is not wet," Ms. Rivers echoes. "So that means there's not a lot of water there. We know that seeds need water, like Camilla started to say. So, if this area,"—she waves at the desert on the page—"if this soil, if this environment, is dry, that means it's not getting the water that it needs. So, let's go back to the question."

Ms. Rivers again points at the page. "Why can't this seed grow in the desert?"

The children raise their hands.

Ms. Rivers leans forward slightly and whispers to the class, "We just talked about it, so you should know. Camilla."

"Because it doesn't have any water," Camilla says.

Ms. Rivers nods her head up and down and smiles slightly. Her eyes widen as she launches into further elaboration: "Right. It doesn't have enough water because it's so dry. Great!" she says as she flashes a thumbs-up sign. "That's how you use what you know," she says as she points to her temple, "and the book"—she points to the page—"to answer a question." Ms. Rivers then continues on to the next part of the story.

This example illustrates one of numerous instances in which Ms. Rivers pushes her students to tackle and persevere through a challenging academic conversation, despite numerous mistakes along the way. They know from the text on the page that the seed is in a dry place, and they know from prior discussions during science lessons that seeds require water to grow. Ms. Rivers hopes that the children can fit together multiple pieces of information to draw a conclusion. After more than 7.5 minutes of intensive back-and-forth exchanges, guesses from six different kindergarteners, three read throughs of the sentence from the book, and multiple restatements of the information, Ms. Rivers eventually gets the group to give the correct answer to her initial question: "How come the seed can't grow?" As I watch the students go back and forth with their teacher in pursuit of the answer, I am both impressed by the level of focus throughout the conversation and taken aback by how Ms. Rivers swiftly and pointedly corrects the children's mistakes. Although the logic of this challenge proves extremely difficult for the kindergarteners to navigate, collectively and with teacher support, the children eventually cobble together a correct verbal articulation of Ms. Rivers's target answer: the desert is hot and dry; dry means there is no water; seeds need water to grow; seeds cannot grow if it is dry.

"STRONG BRAINS. STRONG HEARTS. STRONG TEAM."

Alana Rivers teaches kindergarten at one of Best Charter School's many locations. The campus is new and well maintained, with a beautiful building that is compact in square footage but still feels spacious. As I walk up to the building each morning, the clean lines and shiny surfaces make the building's visage distinct in the mostly residential area. Although it abuts a major intersection, it is not overwhelmingly busy, and the surroundings still feel like a neighborhood where people live. Ms. Rivers's Best Charter campus is situated in the middle of the population it serves: predominantly Black and Latinx students, including a number of first- and second-generation immigrants and English Language Learners (ELL) with emerging English capabilities. A recent annual report conveys that nearly all Best Charter enrollees are people of color, and the vast majority are eligible for free or reduced-price school meals. Serving this demographic supports the school's mission to close the achievement gap and to help children prepare for college through rigorous academic training. As a public charter school network, Best receives state and local funding to fulfill its approved educational mission and operating plan—or "charter"—and is governed by its own guidelines and leadership, independently of the local school district.

The mistake culture in Ms. Rivers's classroom is most certainly shaped by the achievement culture of the broader school environment. Compared to the chronically low academic performance of students at nearby public district schools, Best Charter students excel. High standardized test scores are a point of pride for the school, as Best Charter "scholars"—a common term used to reference the children at the school—rank among the best in the state on several sections of the proficiency exams. Work toward strong and measurable outcomes begins on the first day of kindergarten; and Ms. Rivers shares that at the close of the academic year, her entire class is at or above expectations on the Best Charter School network's grade-level tests.

Rigorous teaching is particularly important to Ms. Rivers because during her time as a Teach for America (TFA) corps member, she "was at a district school where professional development was really a joke." Reflecting back on that very first year in the classroom, Ms. Rivers admits that "I wasn't a good teacher. No one's a good teacher [in their first year]. I didn't do education undergrad." After two years, she decided that "if I want to continue being a teacher, I can't stay here because I'm not going to get better." Best Charter was an attractive option, at least in part, because of the structured training and mentoring they provide that imbues teachers with concrete teaching skills that can move the needle on student performance. When she welcomes me into her classroom, Ms. Rivers is eight years into her teaching career—two in TFA and six in her Best Charter Kindergarten position.

Ms. Rivers and her fellow Best Charter teachers receive a charge at the launch of each school year that is short, sweet, and to the point: "achieve all your goals and get your kids to learn." All teachers must develop a vision for their classroom; and for the past several years, Ms. Rivers has elected to build hers around the idea of "the team." With each visit to her room, I repeatedly observe just how central teamwork is to the logistics of how the class operates. Most activities are done in whole group with cycles of thinking and discussion among the fifteen children who comprise her team; they first take a moment to mentally prepare their own best responses to the given question or task, then swiftly and publicly take turns sharing until someone lands on a correct answer.

For Ms. Rivers, "the team" is at the heart of all learning, and this stance is embodied by her class motto: "Strong brains. Strong hearts. Strong team." Broadly speaking, this goal seems to align with what teachers in other school contexts also pursue with their young pupils. I ask what it means to her, and Ms. Rivers says the motto conveys that "we're growing our brains to get smarter, but we're also caring for each other and learning how to be respectful friends." She says that most children "do not come into kindergarten that way" and considers it her responsibility to help the students grow.

When I ask Ms. Rivers directly about *her* role on the team, she insists that "I don't want them to see me as the leader of the team 'cause I want them to be leaders," but then quickly concedes that she is in charge, given that "I am telling them what to do all day." Although in our conversations Ms. Rivers is reluctant to embrace her leadership role, it seems obvious to me that she truly does operate like a coach. Daily, she prepares her team with direct training, speed drills, and many hours of practice, with the aim that everyone is 100 percent ready to go by game time—be that the next activity, the next test, the next grade level, or college. As I understand it, Ms. Rivers works to overcome the many life factors outside of the children's control that might threaten to derail high academic performance. As their coach, she does not cater to those disadvantages and, instead, pushes them all to perform as elite athletes, no matter what.

Every moment of the day, Ms. Rivers operates as if that big game is coming fast, so the team simply has no time to waste. Within this context, children must give their all during high-stakes practice sessions so that the coach can ensure they have built their endurance and refined their moves enough to give a perfect performance later on, during the game, when it counts the most. Time and again, I watch Ms. Rivers quickly push mistakes and hesitations aside in the class discussion so the team can arrive at the specific, "perfect perfect" response that she has in mind. Coach Rivers makes it clear that she needs everyone to give their all—at all times—and to strive for flawless performance.

The team approach shapes much of Ms. Rivers's teaching style. For instance, speaking together in the team is perceived as a demonstration of engagement and understanding, and I notice that it is a prominent feature of the daily routines in Ms. Rivers's classroom. This includes frequent call-and-response choral recitations in which they chant letter sounds, count numbers, or spell and say their daily sight words, as well as requests for them to read en masse ("Say it with me" while pointing to each word on the board) or celebrate peers ("Say 'she's got it!'" The children respond, "She's got it!"). If the recitation is not crisp and in sync or if some students seem distracted, Ms. Rivers will have the whole team repeat it until everyone says it correctly and with confidence.

Furthermore, "the team" is a concept she references dozens of times a day in her instructional interactions with students, and it directly shapes how she and the children engage with mistakes. Kindergarten children in her class learn that they are individually responsible, not only for their own personal learning but also for their peers' learning. When Ms. Rivers poses a question to the class, it is a charge for each child to "get ready to teach the team." So, every kindergartener strives not only to identify the correct answer to the problem at hand but also to develop a clear explanation that can be shared with others. Their preparedness helps the collective, and Ms. Rivers expects that individual children will remain focused and on task so they can each help pull the team's learning ever-forward toward optimal or "perfect perfect" performance with no mistakes.

COACHING IN CONTEXT: KINDERGARTEN TEACHING AT BEST CHARTER

Best Charter is a well-resourced, multi-campus, public charter school network. It has a sizable support staff, small class sizes, accountability measures for students and teachers alike, and substantial resources from both governmental and private sources. Perhaps one obvious tangible indicator of this is the bounty of supplies in the teachers' lounge in Ms. Rivers's school building. Not only does the spacious and sun-drenched room offer teachers use of a fridge, microwave, and long tables with ports for device charging, but it also contains an entire wall of drawers containing myriad supplies. Along the opposite wall are two frequently used, giant copy machines—one black and white and the other color, the latter a true rarity in U.S., urban, public schools.

Ms. Rivers's classroom layout affords ample space for learning activities, with a rug area for group practice and spacious tables where students complete written work at their assigned seats. A very long wall of tall windows with a view of the playground lets in plenty of light throughout the day. There is a wealth of books in the library, shelf after shelf of learning manipulatives and games in another nook on the opposite side of the classroom, and an area that contains snacks, a few games and toys, and a water table toward the back. Parallel with the door is a small desk where the classroom aide, Miss Thomas, sits for a good portion of the day, occasionally assisting with logistical tasks as requested by Ms. Rivers but, surprisingly, rarely providing instructional support. Along a side wall, just behind the teacher's desk, there is an expanse of bookcases stuffed to the gills with neatly arranged instructional materials and supplies. Ms. Rivers's table is bean-shaped and centrally located in the room; it has her computer, an adult-sized office chair, and several smaller chairs around it.

Ms. Rivers is part of a small group of kindergarten teachers who collectively prepare each week's lessons. She explains that "we have very little box curriculum here" at Best Charter. Instead, they "split responsibilities among the kindergarten team," iteratively refining lessons created during the prior year at this school site because "there's always things you can be making better." They have "co-planning time" built into their schedules for regular meetings to collaboratively improve content and tinker toward ideal lessons. Beyond those meetings, each member of the teacher team takes the lead on preparations for a particular subject or two. Ms. Rivers is in charge of math lessons, so it is her job to "edit them and make sure they are as good as they can be, and then I copy them and distribute them so we're all teaching the same lesson on the same day." Although the teachers do provide additional differentiation for class or individual needs, the teaching team stringently maintains overall alignment of content and pacing.

Furthermore, Ms. Rivers has access to and frequent consultations with specialists who are on campus. In addition to pull-out services for students with specific learning needs, the specialists—including a speech-language therapist and ELL coordinator—are available for "problem solving." For instance, Ms. Rivers explains that "if I have kids in my class . . . who I know I could be serving better, I would go to that expert," who could then provide sound advice for how to appropriately and effectively address student needs.

When it comes to performance, Best Charter School is quite serious about tracking data; rigorous and nuanced assessment is built into the fiber of the place. Ms. Rivers shares that "we do standards-based grades, so I'm not just giving them an A for math." Instead, she utilizes an assessment built on "the Common Core Standards and I grade each one on a zero to four scale." Additionally, students take a number of standardized tests throughout the year. For kindergarten literacy "there's a November, a January, and a June" window during which each child is individually assessed for progress in reading fluency using a running record. Also, math and word study tests are given to all kindergarteners across the campuses of the Best Charter network. The kindergarteners are expected to learn loads of high-frequency sight words or "heart words" that they practice in chunks of fifteen at a time. They review them extensively at school and "then I send home a little note with families" with a list of words to practice before being assessed. This year, the count is up to 160 words as of late April. With the exception of one section on the math test, these tests are all administered one on one by the classroom teacher. In all cases, the Best Charter expectation is strong performance by all kindergarteners.

In addition to student tests, the instructional practices and performance of each Best Charter School teacher are also assessed frequently, with nearly two dozen observations across the year that employ specific rubrics related to professional expectations. After the observations, they have follow-up discussions about the scores—comparing those of supervisors to teacher self-ratings—and these inform the development and tracking of each teacher's short- and long-term goals. Continuous improvement is a priority, and the school invests heavily in an apprenticeship model of teaching, as well as nearly two hundred hours of professional development spread over the course of the year.

This is the context in which Ms. Rivers teaches—a public charter school with ample, tangible resources and supports, as well as demands for consistent and high student achievement. These parameters are essential in shaping how children learn from mistakes in her kindergarten classroom.

KEEP YOUR EYE ON THE BALL: GUARDING TIME AND KEEPING THE TEAM FOCUSED

Ms. Rivers is an unrelenting coach, cultivating her team's ability to focus, listen, and sustain attention so that they can complete academically challenging activities and discussions. As I reflect on this, I can see that successful learning is the most urgent priority in Ms. Rivers's classroom and in the school generally. She explains to me that she feels "you should only be going over things that everyone's getting wrong, because if they all got it right, they already know." With every question, activity, and drill, Ms. Rivers positions being right as the end goal, pushing children to eliminate mistakes.

In the dogged pursuit of rigorous academic standards and correct answers, time is a precious commodity at Best Charter. Ms. Rivers is one of the longest-tenured teachers at the school, admired and well-respected in this community for her teaching abilities. "I've been told that my classroom runs like a well-oiled machine." She goes on to explain, "I don't want to be a dictator, but I do have an expectation for urgency," one of the standards by which she is evaluated during administrative observations of her teaching.

This sense of urgency is palpable in most every moment of the day. Moving slowly and inefficiency are positioned as two of the primary mistakes that Ms. Rivers wants the children to avoid. She pushes the team hard and fast, as a coach would do leading up to a high-stakes tournament. She strives for "no wasted learning time" and frequently conveys the importance of time-on-task, so that the students are clearly aware that "we have things to do." When children move especially slowly, "sometimes I call them grandmas and grandpas" as a reminder that "we don't have time for all of this." Ms. Rivers feels that, at times, the pace is slow because students are "not attending to my directions," and the result is that it interferes with the team's ability to stick to their planned schedule. She further notes that, in particular, "the transitions are where I expect them to be efficient," so the team can shift seamlessly from one activity to the next.

During instruction, I witness Ms. Rivers expend a lot of time and energy correcting behavioral missteps and linking them to academic expectations. If not paying attention, following instructions, or trying their hardest to solve a challenging problem, the children are reminded that being off task is "not really helping the team." If someone fails to recite letter sounds from the wall chart in chorus with everyone else, Ms. Rivers might say to the group, "You all need to look at the wall card to do it right to help the team learn. We'll do it again. Ready, go." If someone does not share a response to an answer in chorus, Ms. Rivers will let them know, "I expect you to be saying what the team is saying."

To that end, this teacher closely, carefully, and constantly monitors student engagement throughout the day, using a "choice stick" as a visual reminder of how each child is behaving at any given moment. The object itself is a yard stick with four distinct color bands (i.e., orange, green, blue, and red), and represents a behavioral continuum that is "supposed to be a reflection of their choices." Each child's name is written on a clothespin that is used to represent their current status. Every morning, each child starts on green, and frequently throughout the day, Ms. Rivers moves individual name clips up to orange or, more commonly, down to blue and red to mirror her assessment of their current behavior status. Most of the time, I see her move children up or down on the stick based on their listening, body posture, and ability to accurately follow directions. Ms. Rivers explains that the color they are on "has nothing to do with me—it's just that I'm reflecting their choices." Although I respect that this is her intention, I do wonder whether this is even possible, as the assessment of whether a child made a behavioral misstep is not black and white like the spelling of a sight word, or the answer to $2 + 2$. Students' choices are necessarily interpreted through the lens of school and teacher expectations. When Ms. Rivers moves names on the choice stick, I see it as a means to enforce the rules and norms that she has predetermined for the children and constituted in the classroom. When packing up at dismissal time, every child must color a square on a calendar in their folders to indicate where they landed at the close of the day. The form is sent home for parents to see daily, adding to its weight and importance. The choice stick factors heavily into the day-to-day teacher-student interactions in the class. Ms. Rivers reaches for it constantly, moving clips up and down and making verbal reminders to keep everyone's conduct on track and efficient in the day's learning activities.

Ms. Rivers usually keeps the flow moving along; however, unanticipated hiccups do slow the team down occasionally. For example, Abraham insists that he needs to go to the bathroom—and "it's an emergency"—right at the very moment Ms. Rivers is beginning a demonstration.

"You can't wait until we're done talking about this?" she asks.

"A little bit," Abraham says meekly.

"Well," she replies, "if you can't wait, you can't wait." Her face is stoic as she shrugs her shoulders slightly. Abraham rises from his spot on the rug and quickly runs out of the room. Ms. Rivers sits silently at the front of the room for a few seconds, as Abraham's footsteps grow increasingly distant, before continuing on with the rest of the team. In this instance, Abraham's exit is ill-timed because it causes him to miss the directions and introduction of new learning. This means that when he returns, he will not know what to do and it may require additional time for him to get up to speed. It would have been more efficient for him to have been there for the presentation, so that he could get the instructions along with everyone else but, in this case, the bathroom break could not wait.

On another occasion, right at the moment the class is about to start an activity, Sumaira shares that she has a paper cut.

"Ouch!" exclaims Ms. Rivers with an empathetic wrinkle of the nose. She politely asks, "Can I help you with that in a few minutes?" but Sumaira wants it sooner. Right away, Ms. Rivers steps away from the front of the room where all of the children stand on their rug spots silent and at attention, prepared and waiting for the next directive.

"Okay," she says to Sumaira, "let's get you a Band-Aid. Come on over."

Sumaira steps out of formation and walks over toward the bean-shaped teacher's desk, behind which the first-aid kit is located.

As Ms. Rivers opens and sifts through the compact, plastic box, she talks gently to the girl about the timing of the interruption. "It would have been helpful before because now the whole team is ready, but we have to wait for you to get a Band-Aid. I'll always give you something that you need, but if you can tell me as soon as you see the problem, that's better for the team." Finally, she finds a bandage and softly hums a little super-hero theme song as she places it carefully on Sumaira's finger. Then, they both return to the rug area and Ms. Rivers launches into the next lesson.

Although Ms. Rivers does not appreciate the ill-timed student requests in these examples, she has a much harsher reaction when she believes students are wasting time. For instance, during one activity, each child already has a slate in hand with a whiteboard surface, and a bucket is going around so they can take a marker and an eraser. When it gets to

Jose, he starts to rifle through rather than simply taking the first one he places his hand on. Ms. Rivers rebuffs this action, saying, "You're moving down." She grabs the choice stick and reaches swiftly for Jose's clip. "All of the erasers are the same. Finding the best one is a waste of your time because they're all the same." Applying my understanding of Ms. Rivers's calculus, I would ascertain that this is a mistake on Jose's part because he slows the pace of passing around the bucket and, by proxy, slows how quickly he and the team can get prepared to learn.

The team format allows for a great deal of efficiency as everyone works together on the same activities at the same pace. I rarely see Ms. Rivers engage one on one with a student to teach something. These are instances in which a student is completely unable to demonstrate a skill during the team practice even though all the rest of the children can. This comes up when Jose is composing a story, but he does not generate all of the required components. He tells Ms. Rivers a fairly long, first pass of a story idea in which he mentions a "dragon," a "tiny wheel," and going to the grocery store. In response, she tells him,

> You don't have a story. You're not ready. . . . You're just saying words. There's no problem. There's no ending. Or beginning. No middle. You're just kinda talking. So, we're gonna work on this together now so that you can tell a story later that makes sense. Like all the books we read; the stories make sense.

Ms. Rivers gives Jose this feedback in a very direct and tough manner that catches me off guard. But, despite the harsh tone, she invests substantial time to make sure he navigates all the steps required for this task. To help Jose, she recounts a story from the class read aloud earlier in the day to model how the story should flow. She listens multiple times as he tries to work through a sequence of ideas, then immediately restates to him what he said and shares how and why it is confusing. On the first day she spends about ten minutes talking with him one on one about this. Then she allots another fifteen minutes the following day, going through a detailed map of the story in which she draws quick representations of the main events so he can reference them later. This is a huge outlay of time, given the pace of the class, but Jose truly does require a lot of support in order to complete this particular writing task.

Just as it is rare for a coach to turn attention away from the whole group right in the middle of practice to pull one player to the side for extensive one-on-one exercises, it is unique for Ms. Rivers to devote this amount of focused attention on one child's individual learning needs. Although she puts in the extra time to provide Jose with this much-needed support, she also repeatedly makes it clear to him that his answers are wrong, do not make sense, and will not work for the assignment. Being pulled out like this is a clear indication that he is making serious mistakes and is not performing at the same level as other children on the team. It also detracts from the overarching goal of efficient learning, which Ms. Rivers and her Best colleagues tend to pursue en masse, rather than in time-consuming, one-on-one check-ins.

LISTEN TO LEARN: KEEPING DISCUSSIONS ON TRACK

Because the school is "discussion-based," Ms. Rivers expects all her kindergarteners to diligently track the thread of the instructional class-room conversations. As she explains, "If this is a whole group, the expectation is that everyone is thinking about the question and trying to figure out the answer." And, when they do provide responses, she wants them to do so confidently. Sometimes she interrupts her students mid-sentence as they are speaking, asking "Can you say it louder?" or she calls out in a strong voice, "Loud and proud so everyone can hear you!" Like a tough, no-nonsense coach, she does not allow members of the team to voluntarily ride the bench, nor to put forward a weak performance during practice sessions. Every rep and drill improves each individual's ability and the team's chances for a future win. Thus, Ms. Rivers wants all members of the team to thoroughly exert themselves, pressing hard all day, every day, in all that the class does.

To stay on task and maximize the team's daily learning, each child is expected to remain fully alert and aware at all times. Ms. Rivers readily acknowledges that it is a sizable developmental challenge to "build their ability to listen to each other, something that five-year-olds don't do." Regardless, the team begins to work toward this from the moment they arrive at Best Charter. Ms. Rivers explains, "The goal for them on the first day of school is to be able to attend to a task for a single minute, and it builds from there." Ms. Rivers makes sure children are attuned to this goal and informs them as they make iterative progress in their time-on-task. To that end, she might give specific feedback to a student: "Wow, you read for five minutes today. Yesterday, you only read for four minutes. Five is more than four; you showed so much focus today."

Gradually, this constant feedback expresses what expected behaviors look like, teaching each individual kindergartener—and the team as a whole—how to demonstrate that they are paying attention. She explains that "we're trying to get them to listen to each other, because that's what you do in high school and college. . . . It's a life skill." She believes that listening is learning, and this plays into her conceptions of what is considered a mistake when the kindergarteners respond. "Discussion is a huge thing we work on as a school; how to support kids to know what a good discussion looks like, sounds like, feels like." She tries hard to get "them to understand what a discussion is" and, for kindergarteners, this requires many prompts from the teacher; she will often "give them a scaffolding question to try to get them there." During classroom discussions, I witness two predominant ways that Ms. Rivers monitors and corrects student focus dozens of times per hour: reminders for body checks and calls to track the speaker.

Ms. Rivers expects students to learn to hold their bodies in specific postures that demonstrate focused listening. "We do a lot of work at the beginning of the year around active listening and what that looks like with your body." They must sit in their assigned seats on the rug with their legs "criss-cross," and she expects that "their hands should not be playing." As a visual reminder, she has affixed to the top of the easel a labeled cartoon image of a child in the active listening stance that she points to as a reminder of the various aspects of active listening: ears listening, eyes looking, mouth quiet, legs criss-cross and still, hands down and still, and brain thinking. Ms. Rivers watches closely to see whether each individual child maintains this posture during all team activities. She calls out "Check your body" or "Let's do a body check" as a means to make public corrections if someone is leaning, fidgeting, or otherwise not meeting the expectation. "I think I'm more on the strict side, but I try to convey meaning to them . . . not just because I need to control you, but because this is how you listen the best." In my time in her class, I watch the students sit on the rug for many hours a day, with smooth and silent transitions between discussions and hands-on practice for various academic content areas. I am amazed that the bulk of the team holds the listening posture in their assigned spots on the rug for as long as ninety minutes at a time, and engages in focused instruction and skills practice with Ms. Rivers for a combined five hours per school day—not even including additional instruction with other teachers during classes like physical education (PE) and foreign language.

Reminders to track the speaker are extremely common in Ms. Rivers's classroom. This is a central part of teaching them how to engage with their peers. When I ask her how it works, Ms. Rivers explains that often "they don't listen to each other when they know they are having a conversation, so we have something called 'track the speaker.'" This means that no one is allowed to sit passively on the rug. Instead, Ms. Rivers wants the kindergarteners to turn their bodies and eyes toward whoever is speaking at a given moment, which she says will help them to follow the thread of conversation. The result of this directive is that, on numerous occasions, I watch as the block of children seated on the floor collectively snap their necks left, right, back, and forth, on and on and on, quickly turning their faces toward the speaker at any given moment. This behavior is by no means spontaneous. "This is a yearlong growth area," and Ms. Rivers builds this capacity in the team slowly over time. They first learn how to track her up at the front of the room. At the start of the year, "the expectation is that you're looking at me or you're looking at whatever we're doing." As the students refine this skill, Ms. Rivers gradually expands the expectation so that they not only track her, but they track anyone who is talking to the team. Ms. Rivers frames tracking the speaker as "doing their job" and, eventually, they are expected to do this as a default without reminders from her.

Based on my observations of class discussions and the children's behavior, I find that the students seem well aware of Ms. Rivers's expectations. However, I am not surprised whatsoever that, as one might expect of young children, it is difficult to get them to perpetually hold their bodies in the expected physical stance of active listening for the entire day. Neglecting to track the speaker during a team-based learning activity is one of the most frequent mistakes the students make in Ms. Rivers's class, as demonstrated by her constant corrections. When focus lapses, she responds with a quick, targeted rebuff: "Nadim, track the speaker," or "Track Charlotte." Children are moved down on the choice stick for not tracking, and Ms. Rivers also will "move people up who are tracking all the time because they're doing their job."

Providing feedback like this actually consumes an extraordinary amount of time in the team's interactions and is at the core of how Ms.

Rivers's classroom operates. She constantly provides feedback to students about their listening and engagement, working very hard to ensure that all members of the team hold their bodies in the correct position, sit on their proper spots, track the speaker appropriately, raise their hands to volunteer answers, and remain silent unless granted permission to speak. During transitions, Ms. Rivers simply tells them where to move, and they almost always get there promptly and with little fanfare. Although I agree that classroom-management techniques are extremely critical to a successful kindergarten class, I have never been in an early childhood context where children's bodies and attention span are monitored to this extent. As I watch, I often wonder to myself whether every child in the class can really receive and respond to her feedback about mistakes in body posture and holding attention, given where they are in their developmental trajectory.

With that in mind, I am aware that one big drawback to this dynamic is that often there are students who demonstrate active listening through their body language without actually paying careful attention to the conversation. Ms. Rivers acknowledges that "some of them are faking until they make it," meaning they raise their hand but then have nothing to say, or do a hand signal to convey that they agree at the "first two words out of [the speaker's] mouth before anything has even been said." In those cases—which happen daily—Ms. Rivers directly calls them out, telling them "you're just pretending" and making sure they know "I can see that you're doing this." In those moments, she reminds the students "you should be waiting to think about what they said." At the heart of it, Ms. Rivers feels the students who do this "want to be seen as participating." However, when they are caught, she expresses her displeasure with this faking and reiterates that this is a mistake, given the class expectations about active listening.

For example, after a lengthy discussion during a math lesson on estimation, one child finally provides a long-awaited correct explanation. Ms. Rivers eagerly invites another team member to repeat it, asking, "What did Nikki just say? 'Cause she had a perfect perfect answer?"

She picks Camilla to share, and although the girl provides some relevant information that is partially correct, it is not the same point that Nikki had articulated.

"I agree with you that four is too small of a number, but that's not actually what she said." Ms. Rivers points at Nikki and asks, "Did you hear what she said?"

Camilla answers her question with a silent no, shaking her head left and right as her black ponytail sways back and forth.

"Then say, 'I wasn't listening,'" directs Ms. Rivers, demanding that Camilla admit her inattention.

With a subtle frown on her face, Camilla looks up at Ms. Rivers and echoes the phrase in a swift admission of guilt: "I wasn't listening."

"Okay," says Ms. Rivers immediately as she strives to keep the conversation moving forward. "Who was listening? Our goal is to listen to our friends so you can learn. If you're not listening, you're not learning. Period."

After this prompt, only one or two hands go up. Hardly any students are willing to offer an answer this go-around. I'm not too surprised, given the reprimand Camilla just received.

Ms. Rivers looks to Nikki. "You're gonna have to repeat it. Not enough people were listening." She then gives a stern charge to the other children, demanding that they all "track her and listen."

In this and countless other moments, I see how Ms. Rivers conveys expectations that the students need to sustain full engagement at all times and carefully track the discussions. Repeating what someone else already said is unacceptable and is framed as a mistake; this is a concept that aligns with school-wide, Best Charter norms for how to actively engage in discussions. Ms. Rivers later explains to me that "it's okay to restate if you're building on, but if . . . your whole answer [is] what someone else already said, you're not contributing to the discussion." In these moments, she immediately brings it to the kindergartener's attention; children are reprimanded for not listening and not helping the class to learn:

- "If you were listening carefully to your friends, you would have heard that both Abraham and Guadalupe already said that. Please don't raise your hand if you're just gonna say the same thing as your friends 'cause that doesn't help us learn."
- "We've already said that. Make sure you're listening to your friends."

In these and numerous other responses, Ms. Rivers conveys the assumption that if the children are not able to provide new information to add to the conversation, if they give a wrong answer to what she considers to be a basic question, or if they cannot repeat what was just said a moment before, then they are not listening.

Ms. Rivers also appears displeased when the team has to cycle through many students to get someone to state the correct answer, or if she has to repeatedly explain things. The natural consequence of the students not listening and staying on task is that "we have less time" to complete other important work, or even to get to fun activities in the day, like shared reading during book buddies or playing games during friendship circles. Responding in the expected manner is a prime goal, and she subtracts time from the more fun and less-structured parts of the day if students cannot get to the right answers within the allocated time for a lesson.

Occasionally, when a student's response is wrong or does not make sense, or if the class is silent, she will ask, "Do you need me to repeat the question?" or she will give permission for a child to request clarity (e.g., "Do you remember what Bilal said? You can ask him to repeat it."). But, in moments like these, I discern from Ms. Rivers's facial expressions, body language, and tone of voice that she is not happy that they are not making more effort to listen to others and track the conversation. Given the high achievement context at Best Charter, her frustration is understandable. However, I can't help but note that her young students' inability to sustain focus for long periods of time, their proclivity to rambling responses, and their difficulties piecing together complex logic actually are normal and widespread behaviors for kindergarten-aged children. Even Ms. Rivers admits on occasion that she demands a lot of five-year-olds, but she never eases up; so, as a coach, she is disappointed at times when the children fail to meet her high standards.

In my observations, Ms. Rivers's team does seem to stay on task as they complete their work together. With constant guidance and correction from their coach, these kindergarteners largely appear to keep their head in the game all day, just as Ms. Rivers and Best Charter demand. As far as I can tell as an observer, I see children who appear to be quite accustomed to these expected norms and know how to "listen to learn" in the manner Ms. Rivers has taught them. However, in my estimation, it is difficult for them to keep it up 100 percent of the time and, developmentally, the effort demands a great deal of very young children—perhaps pushing beyond what many of them can realistically do. Also, it appears that the required moment-to-moment maintenance of this stance is extremely effortful for Ms. Rivers. Although she is good at it, she does have to constantly remind the children—individually and as a team—to stay focused on learning.

EXPECT THE BEST: THE QUEST FOR PERFECT PERFORMANCE AND SELF-CORRECTION

Ms. Rivers holds her kindergarteners to high standards, which includes establishing "the norm that we can fix our own mistakes, if we look for them." She expresses the belief that "striving for no errors is what we want, because that means your brain is growing and you're learning." In practice, I see that Ms. Rivers sets two main priorities in her class: being right and minimizing mistakes. Relatedly, self-determination is highly valued. Ms. Rivers works diligently to teach the students to stick with solving a problem, even if very challenging, until they can self-correct and triumph over it. She is aware of the developmental challenge that this presents for young children. "Most of them—like 90 percent of them— lack that self-awareness of checking their own work. . . . I have to teach them what that exactly means." She does this by providing opportunities and scaffolding to fix their mistakes. That said, she still admits that "giving five-year-olds the self-awareness to find a mistake and fix it without me telling them is like a miracle." But she sees this as a worthwhile investment in their future and knows that "if they can do it before they get to the first grade, they are good to go."

In Ms. Rivers's classroom, it is not enough to approach the right answer; her students must be spot-on, and she decisively probes any misinformation, confusion, or partial understanding until someone on the team develops a precisely correct response. A part of enacting this philosophy about mistakes is that Ms. Rivers is constantly assessing the quality and correctness of the children's performance. When students get answers or explanations exactly right, they often receive unambiguous declarations about the perfection of the answer. This public praise ranges from making a nonverbal hand signal for perfect, to stating directly that a student "had a perfect perfect answer" or did "a perfect job helping" a peer. By contrast, if a child responds incorrectly when Ms. Rivers asks a question that warrants a factual answer, then "my answer will be no, that's not right." Although she may mildly acknowledge the correctness of an individual piece of information, she withholds enthusiastic affirmation of any answer that includes mistakes or omissions and is therefore less than 100 percent correct. In these instances, when the children are wrong, she tends to be extremely brisk and direct in her feedback on their mistakes.

To help students self-correct when they get stuck, she often reminds them of previously discussed strategies they can use to solve the problem. She conveys frequently that strategies are at the heart of what the students are doing and how they can find correct answers for themselves. These function as playbooks that the team can study with the guidance of the coach, for future reference during practice sessions and academic performance. For example, as individual children come up with ideas for how they might solve a problem in math, Ms. Rivers depicts their ideas on chart paper that goes up on the walls as a reference for future discussions. Their names and a smiley face with the child's signature hairstyle accompany an image-based depiction of the math strategy. I think it is pretty clever to generate the ideas from among the children themselves. This could certainly help anchor their insights with a time, place, and person, so that the team can more readily recall and reference each strategy later, when needed. So, if someone does not know what to do, Ms. Rivers might say, "You could use Elizabeth's strategy . . . or you could use Sumaira's strategy." These visual references hearken back to in-depth class discussions and practice activities in which they previously used various approaches to solve math problems.

When someone gets an answer wrong or is confused in the process, she commonly reminds them of their failure to draw on the prior strategies they have previously learned.

- "You're not using a strategy and that's why you're getting them wrong."
- "If you don't know what it is, you can try other strategies. But you can't just keep going. You have to be a listening lion when your brain says, 'That's not right; that doesn't make sense.' You have to go back and try again."

- "I'm not gonna keep checking this if you're gonna keep getting it wrong. You need to use a strategy and figure it out for yourself. Don't show it to me if you think you're getting it wrong."

My takeaway message is that while Ms. Rivers works to give the children what they need to get to the right answer on their own, she also clearly asserts that it is each team member's responsibility to properly recall relevant prior experiences and utilize the many instructional tools at their disposal to avoid mistakes.

This is well illustrated in the lengthy, whole-class discussions Ms. Rivers has with students daily. With her questions and comments, Ms. Rivers provides feedback that prompts the children to reconsider and revise their errors and pushes the onus onto them to stay focused so they can carefully and quickly deduce the right answer. For example, as a part of a math unit on shapes, the team turns their attention to the term *quadrilateral*, a category that includes rectangle, square, rhombus, and all four-sided shapes. In a prior lesson, she defined a square as having four sides and four "perfect" corners that look like the capital letter *L*. In the current activity, Ms. Rivers asks students to identify shapes on flash cards and explain what type of shape it is. At one point, she holds up two flash cards—one of a yellow rhombus and another with a hand-drawn outline of a square—so that the team can identify and compare them.

Charlotte says the shapes are quadrilaterals "because they have four equal sides."

"Nope," says Ms. Rivers. "A quadrilateral is any shape that has four sides." She grabs a whiteboard marker and draws a few more examples for the children to consider, counting the sides for emphasis:

"So, this—one, two, three, four—is a quadrilateral."

"This is a quadrilateral."

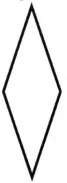

"This is a quadrilateral."

"They're all quadrilaterals because they all have four sides." She holds up the card with the outline of a square on it. "This is a square. It's a special quadrilateral." Ms. Rivers waves the card around and asks, "What's special about this?" Hands go up in the group and she calls on Charlotte.

Charlotte replies, "It's that it has four equal sides."

Ms. Rivers corrects her; "Yep, but," holding up the rhombus card, "so does this. This also has four equal sides. So, why is this a square?"

"Because it has four perfect corners," Charlotte says matter-of-factly, "not too big or too small."

Ms. Rivers directs the class: "Say, 'She's got it.'"

The class echoes the affirmation. "She's got it!"

In this exchange, Ms. Rivers directly tells Charlotte that she is incorrect, and provides detailed explanations and examples to ensure that she makes it to the right answer by the end of the interaction. When she does get it, she gets a resounding affirmation from her coach and teammates: "She's got it!"

Another approach that Ms. Rivers uses to help the team correct a mistake is to urge them to provide more information, either by giving an open-ended prompt, or asking a question. For example, during a science activity, she wants the team to tell her how to plant a seed, one step at a time. She asks for someone to share what to do first, so that she can write a list on a large sheet of chart paper.

"We should put soil," offers Elizabeth.

"Put soil," says Ms. Rivers, writing the words on the chart paper. Then she looks at Elizabeth. "Put soil, put soil . . ." She stands in silence for four seconds, lips pursed as she looks around at the class. Hands dart into the air, poised to build on Elizabeth's response. Ms. Rivers points to a peer.

"Put the soil . . ." Charlotte pauses for a moment before proceeding. ". . . in the container," she finishes.

Ms. Rivers points to Elizabeth and asks, "Is that what you meant?" She turns back to her chart paper and says the words as she writes them down. "Put the soil in the container. That's a little more information. Now I know exactly what to do. Put the soil in the container."

In this interaction, Ms. Rivers does not tell Elizabeth she is wrong, but instead she pauses to make space for the team to correct the response. Although Elizabeth does not correct herself, she still will get to access the detailed directions Ms. Rivers writes on the chart paper that will later guide the team as they plant their seeds.

COACH-LED CORRECTIONS: DIRECT TEACHER ASSESSMENT

In many of Ms. Rivers's team discussions, the pathway to the right answer is circuitous and rife with the children's mistakes and missteps, and they cannot self-correct. In those cases, she is more heavy-handed in her efforts to try to steer the children back in the right direction. Frequently, in lieu of content- or task-specific corrective feedback, Ms. Rivers offers commentary on the type of response the kindergartener has given. For example, if a child is talking in circles and/or the response is difficult to follow, she will restate the child's answer verbatim with a puzzled look (e.g., shrugged shoulders and a furrowed brow) or say directly that the answer does not make sense. During one particularly challenging and incredibly lengthy math conversation, Camilla works to correct and extend a response a peer has just made. She rocks back and forth in her spot and subtly shrugs her shoulders as she softly speaks her answer for almost sixty seconds. From where I sit, it is hard to hear; her body language and tone of voice as she gives her winding answer convey that she may be unsure of what she's sharing. I turn my attention back to Ms. Rivers to find she is holding her forehead with her fingers. She suddenly raises her head and abruptly interrupts Camilla's response.

"Camilla," says Ms. Rivers in a soft whisper and with a strained smile. "I can't understand what you're saying the more you talk about it." Her tone of voice sounds like a mix between tired and frustrated as she asks, "Do you have something to say or are you not ready?" She looks up at the girl, with a stern look on her face.

"I have something to say," says Camilla softly.

"We would love to know what it is," urges Ms. Rivers in a hushed voice as she continues to look at Camilla. "But you're not making any sense. Would you like to start again? That's a good strategy. Track Camilla."

This exchange with Camilla is one of many wrong answers in an extremely fraught conversation during which child after child gets close to stating a 100 percent accurate response but falls short, again and again. Ms. Rivers's tone with the children is curt and, as I watch, I wonder if it would be worth it for the team to take a little time away from this and loop back later—maybe even the next day—to let the intensity cool down. But despite the difficulties, Ms. Rivers keeps pressing through until eventually one of the children does provide a correct statement. The team is stuck repeatedly making mistakes while discussing the same math concept for almost fifty minutes across three separate sessions that day (from ten to thirty-two minutes each), plus an additional fifteen minutes at the end playing a game to practice applying the skill. This is a shockingly long time for kindergarteners to work on a single topic in a given day. Later, once the children leave the room, even Ms. Rivers readily admits to me that she did not lead this lesson well, and she probably should have moved on from this sooner. However, I do not hear her say this to the children and, in the arc of this exchange, she tells more than one of them that their mistakes don't make sense.

Another way that Ms. Rivers redirects children's mistakes is with the feedback that a response does not address the question asked. She explains to me that there is an "expectation that they should be listening to the question," but she acknowledges that "part of the kindergarten struggle is responding to the questions really asked, not just a tangent." Ms. Rivers works to keep them focused on the task at hand and gives little leeway for meandering answers. Through her words and actions, she makes it clear that a tangential answer that is factually correct but irrelevant to the question is wrong.

One day during the literacy block, I watch as the children look at a sentence and discuss the use of capital letters. On a sheet of chart paper posted in the front of the class are some sentences that Ms. Rivers has just written for them to consider:

We look at the speaker. My body is calm and focused. My hands are down and still.

Ms. Rivers stands in front of the room and calls on Marisol to answer her question: "Why does this *M* have to be a capital letter but not any of the other letters?" She folds her hands and looks down at Marisol as she starts to respond.

The child begins: "Because, because . . ." Ms. Rivers snaps her fingers at other children, gesturing for them to pay attention as Marisol responds. ". . . because, because capital letters are in the top space."

"Yes," says Ms. Rivers, "but that doesn't answer my question." There is a short stretch of silence across the room as her feedback settles. Shaking her finger at Marisol, Ms. Rivers clarifies, "I didn't say 'How do I make a capital letter?' or 'How do you know it is a capital letter?' I said"—Ms. Rivers points at the capital *M* in the word *My*—"'Why should this be a capital letter, but all of these should be lowercase?'" She slides her finger along the balance of the sentence.

Marisol continues to stutter as she searches her mind for an answer. "Be-because. Because." Three more seconds of silence pass as Ms. Rivers smiles at her. "Because."

Ms. Rivers points up at the sentence again. "Why should this *M* be a capital letter?"

"Because . . ." Marisol trails off into two or three more seconds of silence. She is frozen.

Ms. Rivers finally intervenes. "Just say, 'I need help.'"

Marisol immediately obliges. "I need help."

"Okay," says Ms. Rivers. She pauses, as hands go in the air from children who are willing to help out. "Can you call on someone, Marisol?" Marisol picks Sumaira.

Sumaira answers correctly. "Because that's the first letter in your sentence."

Ms. Rivers looks out at the children as she echoes and elaborates Sumaira's answer. "This period," she says, pointing, "means this is a new sentence. I'm saying something new; saying something about my hands. So that first letter has to be a capital letter."

Marisol's mistake here is that she veers off track and shares general information about writing capital letters rather than answering the question asked. It is almost like the coach asked for someone on the team to demonstrate a jumping jack and, when called upon, Marisol started doing push-ups—her action does not meet the coach's demands. Although both exercises require exertion, they do not flex the same muscles or demonstrate the same capability.

If a kindergartener is heading down a confusing tangent, Ms. Rivers does not hesitate to interrupt—abruptly stopping them from proceeding with their response—and immediately move on to someone else. By saying "No," or more directly, "I'm gonna stop you," she cuts off the children mid-sentence when they are headed down a tangent that is "confusing" or shifts away from the right answer. This is all done in the team formation, on the rug, with everyone watching and following along with every step. Sometimes the answers come from multiple attempts by different children as they try to produce a response; but occasionally, Ms. Rivers will volley back and forth with one student.

In one instance, Abraham keeps mixing up his use of the words *before* and *after* during a math-practice game in which the group is broken out into two teams—"Art Kinder" and "Kinderlightning"—that are competing for points. Art Kinder is ahead, and now Kinderlightning—Abraham's team—has a chance to try to catch up. After establishing in a prior question that the number 14 comes before the number 15, Ms. Rivers has now asked, "How do you know that 14 is before 15?" referencing a number sentence written out on the board: *14 is before 15.* Ms. Rivers calls on Abraham, leaning her chin on the slate that is propped up on her lap, as she watches and attentively listens to him. He tries hard to make a statement about the relationship between the two numbers on the board but keeps mixing up his wording.

"Because I know 14 is . . . is after; 14 is after . . ." Tentatively stuttering through his opening, he then pauses and seems to be thinking.

"Abraham, come on," nudges Ms. Rivers, pushing him to recalibrate his answer.

"14 is after . . ." He trails off again.

"Abraham!" Ms. Rivers waves the marker under the word *before*, written up on the whiteboard, to provide a more direct signal that he has made a mistake.

He looks up and sees her waving under the number sentence. "Oh. Before. Before 14 . . ."

Ms. Rivers interrupts to calmly reiterate the math statement written on the board that he is trying to explain: "14 is before 15."

He repeats and extends the answer: "14 is before 15 and I know that because 5 is before, 5 is before 4." He stops, looking up at her for verification.

Ms. Rivers, who is still resting her chin on the slate, closes her eyes for a moment, and then looks up at Abraham again. "But it's not," she says meekly, followed by a three-second pause of silence as the feedback sinks in. She raises her head and further explains: "5 doesn't come before 4. You're getting confused with the words *before* and *after*."

Abraham gives a quick nod of affirmation.

"You understand what to do. You're just not saying the right words. Can you try one more time? Why is 14 before 15?"

After a few moments to collect himself, Abraham takes another crack at it. "Be-Because." Another seven seconds of silence pass. Ms. Rivers tells Nadim to put his hand down as Abraham continues to formulate his answer. The team sits in silence, waiting for him to piece together a revised response.

"Because . . ." Another five seconds of dead air pass. There are no interruptions for Abraham's think time; everyone waits.

Ms. Rivers urges him to wrap up his answer. "You have to try to get the point."

"Because . . ." he starts again, and pauses for another seven seconds, before picking up the answer again: "4 . . . 4 is." Five seconds of silence.

Then, out of the quiet he yells, "4 is!" He swallows the end of the sentence.

"Nadim, put your hands down," says Ms. Rivers, giving a quick "body check" to this wiggly child who is rocking and waving his hands right beside Abraham, perhaps a bit impatient as he waits for his peer to finish: "4 is behind."

"Abraham," Ms. Rivers interjects, "the words are *before* and *after*."

"4 is before 5."

"Got it!" shouts Ms. Rivers. She promptly heralds his triumph with a strong voice and a straight face: "Two points! For showing self-determination when it was tricky. Nice job, Abraham." The team then immediately moves on to the last question in the game.

I agree—this certainly is tricky! From my view on the sidelines, I am not sure whether Abraham will piece this answer together; he has me biting my nails right up to the last second. This exchange takes two minutes total—not a very long time on the clock—but it feels quite lengthy from my perspective sitting in the room, as there are a great many silent pauses, stutters, and incorrect answers from Abraham, and redirecting comments from Ms. Rivers. Yet, even as other children are eager to speak, Ms. Rivers holds space for Abraham to puzzle through to the right answer without passing the baton to someone else on the team. As his coach, she gives Abraham the chance to get much-needed practice with this concept and to flex his academic muscles so that he can prepare for success in future matches with this content.

TRYING REQUIRED, NOT OPTIONAL: THE TEAM MUST PLAY TO WIN

Ms. Rivers's team knows that trying hard means listening, staying engaged, and preparing to provide (correct) responses quickly, whenever prompted. In her words, actions, and tone of voice, Ms. Rivers conveys that it is unacceptable to remain silent when asked to generate a response; disengaging or being passive are huge mistakes in her classroom. One day, she has a private conversation with Min after the other children are dismissed to their tables to start some seatwork. I overhear her in a whispered hush, as she sharply scolds him for keeping his hand down during the prior lesson. Through her subsequent comments, she appears to interpret his lack of engagement as withdrawal from the learning experience:

> When I ask you to talk, you have to talk. You have a responsibility to the team to teach them what you know. It's not okay to pretend that you don't understand. I know that you do understand. It's not okay that you're pretending that you don't. Or, if you do feel confused, you need to listen well. Instead of playing with your fingers. So, we're gonna practice listening and talking now.

In my interpretation, this feedback indicates that silence and inaction are unacceptable. In her remarks, Ms. Rivers conveys confidence in Min's ability to complete the task and clarifies that "listening and talking" are the only acceptable ways to participate—NOT silence.

In a different instance, Ms. Rivers asks Marisol to explain her rationale for her correct answer to a question during math practice. Rather than delve into fine-grained details of how she solved the problem, Marisol says various iterations of "I know because I used my brain." It doesn't land well with Ms. Rivers at the onset. As Marisol says it two additional times, interspersed with a couple of unclear and/or incorrect explanations, Ms. Rivers eventually loses patience with this answer, cuts her off, and sternly redirects her.

"Marisol, stop saying you used your brain. You have to talk about the numbers. You used all these strategies yesterday. You were here yesterday. You were part of this conversation." She points at the large pieces of white paper with drawings and notes that reflect the ideas developed by the children during the math lesson on the prior day. "You can use Nikki's strategy and count. You can use Elizabeth's strategy and use the number line." As Ms. Rivers talks to Marisol, the other children are absolutely silent, seated on their spots, tracking the conversation throughout. "You have to talk about a tool or a strategy that you are using. You can't just say,"—raising her arms, and talking in a high-pitched voice—"'I just know, I know in a snap.'" Ms. Rivers drops her shoulders and shakes her head *no* as she looks at Marisol. "You can't say that. You have to talk about something." Ms. Rivers reaches out her hand toward Marisol, inviting another try. "How do you know?"

Although she constantly talks about how the team must "use their brains" to solve challenging problems, this phrase alone is not an adequate explanation without further detail to back it up. Ms. Rivers's comment clearly indicates that this is an unacceptable response, and she insists that Marisol must provide a detailed, content-based explanation to justify her answer. Often, I see Ms. Rivers prompt this from children mid-discussion by asking them to finish the phrase "I know because . . . ," offering an additional opportunity to try to explain their thinking. They are expected to fill in the blanks.

After this particular instance, Ms. Rivers continues to ask Marisol questions for more than two minutes, pushing her to select one of the strategies developed by the class in a prior lesson and to use it as the basis of a verbal rationale that explains her answer. I am amazed at the resilience that Marisol shows throughout the exchange, as she receives very direct feedback about the imprecision of her language and is asked again and again to self-correct her errors. I think children typically would be upset or in tears by now, and even many adults would not take this intense dissection of their mistakes very well. But Marisol does stick with the task at hand and, with substantial prompting, eventually crafts a cohesive response, at which point Ms. Rivers instantly declares, "You're a star, Marisol! That was amazing. Shooting stars for Marisol—one, two, three." Just as teammates and coaches cheer their personal triumphs and victories, the teacher and all of the other children clap and make a "psh" sound as their fingers rain down, emulating fireworks as a means for them to briefly celebrate Marisol's success before immediately moving on to the next thing on the agenda.

In Ms. Rivers's class, raised hands are considered a clear demonstration of active engagement and effort toward reaching the correct answer. She explains, "If they think they might know, they should be raising their hand to try; but if they don't know, they should be ready to listen to the person who does." However, when watching Ms. Rivers's responses to students when they make mistakes or fail to raise their hands, I notice that the children do face a dichotomous teacher response that they must very carefully navigate.

On one hand, Ms. Rivers expects them to raise their hands so they can try to provide responses to her questions. Often, she explicitly says things like "if your hand is up it means you found the answer," indicating that all students should know the correct response to the question being asked. If she does not feel that enough hands are raised, she sometimes pauses before moving forward, telling the team she is "waiting for more hands" or "I should see more hands." On the other hand, Ms. Rivers indicates that she absolutely does not want students to raise their hands if they do not have a well-thought-out answer. I observe several occasions in which a kindergartener fumbles when called on by the teacher, repeating information that a classmate already stated, tentatively giving an incorrect answer, stating "I don't know," or simply saying nothing. Ms. Rivers's visceral response is similar across all of these instances: unambiguous displeasure and frustration. Repeatedly, she says things like "I don't really know why you raised your hand," "If you don't know, just leave your hand down," or "Please only have your hand up if you're ready to be a teacher." Whether it is a lack of confidence, a moment of conceptual confusion, or a temporary lapse in attention, the children do not always know the correct answer and/or sometimes lose track of the thread of the conversations.

If Ms. Rivers feels a child is being deceptive—that is, purposely pretending to know and raising a hand to blend in with the class—she calls them out directly. On one such occasion, she pauses the group discussion to redirect a child who raises a hand up high in the air for a moment, and then shyly holds it up next to her face. Ms. Rivers sees this and motions for her to put her hand down. "If you don't know, don't raise your hand. You don't need to raise your hand. It's okay that you don't know—that's why we talk about it together. But don't pretend." Ms. Rivers puts her hand up next to her face and glances up at the ceiling, acting as if she is timidly raising her own hand to share. "You're not fooling me," she quips with a little smile, before moving on to the next child with a hand raised high. This also comes up when students are asked to "whisper to your hand"—a common strategy Ms. Rivers uses to help students think about and practice verbalizing their answers before they share them out loud with the team. Regularly, she catches children who have been clearly whispering into their hands but then have nothing to say immediately afterward. She does not appreciate this behavior and addresses it directly: "You all were just talking to your hand so you should have something to say." In either case, she makes it clear that pretending to engage in the learning is entirely unacceptable.

I also frequently witness moments in which Ms. Rivers expresses disappointment that students are not reaching the answers more quickly.

Sometimes she implies that they are not trying hard enough, explicitly saying that she feels her questions are not that challenging.

- "It's not that hard of a question."
- "You're thinking a little too hard about this."
- "Friends, these directions actually aren't that difficult. I'm a little confused about why you don't know."
- "Your job is to think. What comes after that number? That's it. It's not difficult."

In most cases, the team is taking a long period of time to state what she considers to be a simple or uncomplicated fact. Despite her perceptions of how easy it is, they do not quickly land on the right answer, so time is passing and their progress is stymied. As I observe, I must admit I am startled to hear the tone and word choice that Ms. Rivers uses in many of her comments about these mistakes and misunderstandings, particularly given the fact that these are young children in their first year of formal education. In these moments, the message to the kindergarteners is that they should only raise their hand if they feel very confident about their answers. I wonder about the impact on their willingness to lean into intellectual risk-taking if it were not required and facilitated by the teacher. How will this foundation laid in kindergarten impact their engagement with learning later in their academic lives? Will it make them eager and confident participants, or will they shirk challenges when given the option? Only time will tell.

On a few, rare occasions, Ms. Rivers directly acknowledges the level of challenge when children make common mistakes, explicitly telling the kindergarteners that—despite their good efforts—something is especially "tricky" to figure out because it defies standard conventions. This comes up one morning when the students are trying to say the date and Camilla says it is the "Twenty-oneth." A majority of the children make the "I agree" hand signal, indicating they think her answer is right.

After a pause, Ms. Rivers affirms Camilla's effort but makes clear this is not right. "I agree that the number should be twenty-one. Does anyone know what we would say for that? Because twenty-oneth—that was a really good try," she says, raising her eyebrows, "but it's not what you would say," she explains with a shake of the head.

When the next student guesses "twenty-one," Ms. Rivers says in a calm and understanding voice, "It *is* the number twenty-one." She confirms this particular fact, nodding her head yes. Then she points at the board and continues to give an additional clarification. "Remember, in the date we say March 1st, March 2nd, March 3rd; not March 1, March 2, March 3." After these elaborations, Guadalupe, the third respondent, finally gets it right.

"You got it," says Ms. Rivers. "March 21st." She shakes her head left and right. "I know it's crazy, I don't know why we do that. We should just say twenty-one but it's twenty-first. Good try though."

In this example, Ms. Rivers directly acknowledges that the right answer is not intuitive. She is supportive of their efforts, readily asserting that their incorrect answers make sense because the correct answer is not easy to produce or remember. These are approaches I have seen in other kindergarten classrooms—the acknowledgment that the children are tackling tricky tasks and spelling conventions that defy logic and are impossible to explain, given their prior knowledge. Although moments like this are rare in Ms. Rivers's classroom, they do provide some additional insights into her assessment of the children's efforts, and her perceptions of the task challenge level.

HEAD TO HEAD: MODELS AND COMPARISONS TO EMPHASIZE RIGHT AND WRONG

Sometimes Ms. Rivers tries to push her team to think beyond correcting mistakes, landing on a particular answer, or articulating what they understand. Just as a coach would give notes when a player makes a move using the improper form, she occasionally wants to tease apart what is wrong about something so that the team can avoid the mistake in the future. During my time in her class, I observe a few instances in which she holds up a potential response and asks students to explain why it is *not* a good answer or approach. For example, when the class is doing an estimation game in which the children try to guess how many cubes she is holding, she engages Jose in an exchange about the answer "zero."

She has some cubes in hand, snapped together into a bar. Each child has a whiteboard and marker, and Ms. Rivers asks the team members to individually estimate and then write down how many cubes they think she is holding. Afterward, they count them and figure out that there are three. Ms. Rivers then poses a question: aside from the number three, "what other numbers would be the best guess?" She calls on Jose.

"Umm," he hesitates, his eyes darting left and right as he searches for a response. "Zero," he says, shrugging slightly as he gazes up at the teacher.

"Zero would be a good guess for how many cubes I have here?" asks Ms. Rivers.

After a couple of seconds, Jose replies, "No."

"No. Why not Jose?"

"'Cause that's nothing," he reiterates, straight-faced.

There's a second or two of silence, as Ms. Rivers starts to nod her head up and down. "Yeah. So why would it be a bad guess?" she asks.

Jose replies, "Because that means you have nothing," shrugging at the end of his response.

Ms. Rivers nods and smiles at Jose to affirm this statement, then looks around at the team as she explains. "And I have cubes, right? So, if I held up cubes to you and then you wrote zero, that would probably be the worst guess that you could make. Because we know that there are *some* cubes, not *no* cubes." She then turns back to Jose with one final piece of feedback. "If I ask a question," she says, widening her eyes and raising her hand as Jose did earlier, "and then I call on you and it kind of just leaves your brain,"—she makes a motion from her head toward the ceiling—"instead of making a silly guess, you can just say, 'I don't know.'" Her face is neutral as she makes this final point, and she stares at him directly. Jose cradles his slate, staring back at her for three seconds. "Why don't you try that now?" suggests Ms. Rivers, breaking the silence.

"I forgot," admits Jose.

"Okay, I'll call on somebody else." She reiterates the question so others can answer, and the team quickly goes on to identify four and two as the two other best guesses you could make.

In this interaction with the team and throughout the lesson, I watch as Ms. Rivers draws attention to strategies students can use to avoid wrong answers, namely, applying logic and prior knowledge to improve their estimation skills. She is not shy about pointedly and promptly telling Jose he is wrong and refers to the answer he provides as "the worst guess." But still, she does have moments of affirmation as he changes course to correct his answer. Ms. Rivers leverages Jose's mistake as a teachable moment; she highlights the flaw in his logic so that he and others can circumvent missteps like this later, and also conveys that he should think carefully and avoid a "silly guess" like this in the future. Throughout the exchange, Jose's facial expression is neutral, and he replies to each request of the teacher quickly and without emotion. As an observer, I wonder whether he is holding in a reaction in response to being called out for his mistake. Is he truly acclimated to his wrong answers being dissected publicly? Does he mind that Ms. Rivers called his response "the worst" and "silly"? Looking at him, I simply cannot read his emotionless face or his body language.

During other efforts to push the team toward perfect performance, Ms. Rivers looks for opportunities to compare and contrast the strengths and weaknesses of her students. These moments remind me of intense, intra-squad scrimmages during which a coach pits half of the team against the other half, in an attempt to intensify the rigor and stakes of the practice. I witness this at a couple of points during my time in her class. One day students sit at her desk one by one to take a standardized assessment on their knowledge of letter-sound "chunks"—for example, digraphs like *sh* and *ch*. Before they start, she tells each child about the performance of specific peers: "Sumaira and Jose both got 100 percent on this because they looked at all the chunks and went really slow. You ready to get 100 percent, too?" At the end of her assessment with each kindergartener, Ms. Rivers affirms perfect performance by saying, "Guess what? 100 percent. Great job. Thank you so much," or "100 percent. Great job."

On this particular assessment, just three of her students got less than 100 percent. At the end of their tests, they receive very different feedback on their performance than the other students. To Marisol, Ms. Rivers says, "There are some chunks you don't know. So, you're going to have to learn them. When we're doing the wall cards, make sure you're looking so you can learn those chunks. Maybe next time 100 percent. Not today." Ms. Rivers reminds other children of their past inattention during the recitations of letter sounds on the wall cards. She explains to Min, "You only got 50 percent because there were some chunks you missed. You weren't looking at the wall cards. You have to listen to the team." In these instances of making mistakes on the assessment, Ms. Rivers tells the children in no uncertain terms that it is their past actions and choices that have led to their underperformance on the present task. She frames it as their personal responsibility, while also telling them a concrete way to improve future performance: look and pay attention during team practice.

Another way she compares students to each other in an effort to motivate performance is by using the work of a few students as a model for the rest of their teammates, who are trying to assess their own work or progress. As Ms. Rivers explains, "I do that at times where I need them to see similarities or differences between their work, or if I need them to evaluate each other's work." For example, a comparison like this comes up when the students are preparing idea webs to plan a writing composition. Charlotte and Guadalupe both sit next to Ms. Rivers in chairs, up at the front of the room, papers in hand. Charlotte is the first to read her story aloud; the team's "thinking job" is to assess whether she provided the required detail in her explanations. Ms. Rivers does intermittent checks with the team, and the children confirm that she did explain each of the three points planned out in the idea web. After she's finished reading, Ms. Rivers says, "Say 'Thanks, Charlotte.'"

The team echoes in chorus, "Thanks, Charlotte." Charlotte is smiling, still holding up her idea web, as Ms. Rivers holds up the story text and continues with instructions for the class.

"If you are like Charlotte and you are done with your writing, and you know that you explained all of the reasons on your web, you need to draw your picture and color it." She holds up Charlotte's paper toward the children and asks, "Is this picture finished? Show Charlotte a thumb."

The room is silent as the majority of the team gives a thumbs-down or thumb to the side, indicating that they do not agree with the statement. As I watch Charlotte look around the room, her smile melts into a more neutral pose, and then the corners of her mouth push downward into a slight frown.

Ms. Rivers poses a question for help from the team. "Who can tell me why it's not finished? Mateo."

"She didn't color it," offers Mateo.

Ms. Rivers raises her palms and echoes this point of feedback. "Didn't color it." As the teacher turns toward Charlotte to provide her with more feedback in front of the class, Charlotte quickly starts smiling again. Ms. Rivers points to a nearby reference poster and reads the first line: "Careful coloring makes sharp pictures even better." Charlotte stands and looks at it as Ms. Rivers reads the rest of it to her and the team. "There's the poster. 'Use colors that look like real life. Color inside the lines. Fill up all the white space.' Got it?" Ms. Rivers turns back toward Charlotte and holds the paper out to her.

"Got it," says Charlotte in a soft voice, smiling as she takes the paper from her teacher.

Over the span of the interaction, I watch Charlotte's countenance shift—from a smile to a frown—as she realizes that none of the team has given her the thumbs-up that indicates her picture is done. And then, surprisingly, her mouth turns into a smile again as Ms. Rivers turns toward her to give final notes on how to improve. I don't know how Charlotte is responding on the inside, but reading her body language, I sense that she may be disappointed that she made a mistake by forgetting the final step to finish her work.

Charlotte returns to her chair up front. Then, Ms. Rivers and the class listen to Guadalupe read her paper and they examine her illustration and writing.

"She did such a good job explaining her reasons," says Ms. Rivers, reaching to take her illustration. "If you're like Guadalupe and you're done explaining all the reasons on your web, *and* you're finished coloring your picture, then you get to move on. She's totally done." To solidify the point, she asks the team one last question: "Do you notice the difference between Guadalupe's work and Charlotte's work?" I notice that Charlotte, from her seat up front facing the class, starts smiling again and gives a quick nod of agreement as she is mentioned in the explanation. "Guadalupe is totally done. Charlotte's not done yet. She's not done with her picture. Say 'Thanks, Guadalupe'"

In chorus, the class echoes, "Thanks, Guadalupe."

Everyone gets back to work on their projects.

Reflecting on these moments, I find Ms. Rivers's comparisons of student work—to the correct answer or to other children's responses—to be the most foreign to my personal teaching experience and my observations of other classrooms. I am used to seeing individual student work—especially on assessments—kept private, with model work held up before the class and bigger mistakes handled discreetly, gently, and individually. From what I witness during my time at Best Charter School, I conclude that this is not Ms. Rivers's way. She is bold and confrontational and truly does not hold back in her critique of children's mistakes. Watching this, I yearn to know more about the inner emotion behind Jose's stoic face and Charlotte's fading smile in these moments of being called out in front of the group. Although the children may be accustomed to Ms. Rivers's style of providing this feedback, I wonder what orientation toward mistakes this establishes and how it will impact their future engagement with learning and taking risks.

COACHING FOR RESULTS, BUT AT WHAT COST?

> We try to plan for mistakes and use them as teaching tools, as opposed to looking at correct answers, because we think that that normalizes error.
> —Ms. Rivers

I conclude my time in Ms. Rivers's kindergarten classroom conflicted. Undoubtedly, she is an enthusiastic host and a thoughtful educator, who is well trained by her charter network and who approaches her teaching intentionally. I am genuinely curious about her way of responding to the children's mistakes, but a number of her methods run counter to my experience and training in early childhood learning and teaching, and to generally accepted norms in the field. I know that the goal at Best Charter is college attendance, but not all of Ms. Rivers's strategies for providing feedback and prompting class discussion emulate those most professors use in university settings. In particular, the affective responses that she has to children's mistakes are beyond what I see adults even use with each other.

Ms. Rivers is a very tough coach who wants her team to produce right answers promptly and with minimal mistakes along the way. The juxtaposition between the thoughtful approach to instruction that she articulates when we talk one on one during our interviews versus the negative emotion that I sense regularly when she enacts her theory in practice are difficult to reconcile.

When I take a step back to consider the environment at Best Charter, it puts Ms. Rivers's methods into context. The larger-than-life reality of the achievement gap looms over day-to-day instruction, motivating Ms. Rivers and her Best Charter colleagues to use what might be considered by some extreme and unconventional methods to get results. There is no time to waste, because the school seeks to overcome, in some cases, generations of past disadvantages—hurdles that could impede their quest to prepare children for college.

In my interpretation, the achievement gap is positioned as the high and intolerable result of complacency, inaction, and the status quo—something Best teachers work to help their students avoid. The upside to her methods is that Ms. Rivers truly coaches her students to be excellent. They attain high levels of academic achievement on standardized tests with few or no mistakes, and the majority do learn how to demonstrate at least the appearance of focus during discussions, even at the very tender ages of five and six years old. The downside is that this strong achievement may come at the cost of the affective elements of teaching and community. During one of our interviews, Ms. Rivers says, "We want them to feel good about getting things right, but we want them to feel better about new understanding. Learning how to do something right when you previously did it wrong is much more valuable." I agree with this sentiment, but when I see it enacted in her class, I am left wondering if there's room for good feelings in these moments of learning from mistakes. Perhaps the intense focus on right over wrong obscures the joy that can come from the journey to understanding and discovery.

3

MISS CARRIE

Guiding Children Down the Highway
to Self-Correction

The greatest sign of success for a teacher . . . is to be able to say, "The children are now working as if I did not exist."
–Maria Montessori

Work time in Carrie Smith's Montessori classroom is always characterized by a flurry of child-driven activity. For many hours a day, young children work in every nook and cranny of Miss Carrie's large classroom, engrossed in a myriad of self-directed activities. Some sit on the floor hunched over small mats, while working with neatly arranged materials. Some stand at easels painting, mixing colors, and creating works of art. Some wash tables, scoop small beads, or eat snacks. Still others sit at child-sized tables writing or drawing, arranging cards or objects, or talking with a peer about a project. Adding to the movement and energy is the presence of constant sound. The background noise is comprised of an eclectic mix of sources: chairs bumping and scraping when pulled in and pushed out from tables, shoes shuffling across the floor, objects tapping against hard surfaces, instrumental music playing softly, and children's voices. The clamor of the room hums along all morning; not so loud as to be distracting but too loud to ignore.

Day after day, I observe that the main thrust of exertion in Room 132—Miss Carrie's classroom—comes from the children themselves.

The children make decisions about where to work, who to work with, and what to do next, using teacher-provided instructional materials to make choices and assess their own progress as they go along. As the children buzz about on their own, Miss Carrie is also hard at work in their midst. Whether teaching a child how to do a new activity, marveling at a student's hard-earned moment of success, or providing feedback on how to improve an independently-generated work product, Miss Carrie assumes a supportive role for the children as they pursue their personal pathways to learning. She rarely draws the students together into whole or small groups to complete teacher-selected tasks—as is common in more traditional classrooms. Instead, Miss Carrie constantly steps around the room to sit and work in different locations, rapidly shifting her attention from one person to the next throughout the children's daily work time. In these interactions, I witness that she and her students confront many mistakes and misunderstandings.

Every day, Miss Carrie dresses professionally but comfortably, as she is always on the move around her classroom. During my observations one morning, I look up and see Sienna standing next to her teacher. The small girl wears a navy dress; her wide, black curls flow down her back and over her shoulders. Miss Carrie is a White woman of medium height with short brown hair, long enough to be pulled back out of her face into a tiny bun atop her head. Today, she is dressed in dark gray capri pants, a short-sleeved white shirt made of a flowy, linen material, and open-toed sandals. The pair walk over to a shelf and Miss Carrie pulls out a stack of stapled papers. Eventually the two sit together on a bench for about a minute, flipping through the pages of Sienna's in-progress story about when she got a shot at the doctor's office. At the close of their brief chat, Miss Carrie sends Sienna on her way, saying, "You can put the story in and I can help you organize it, okay?"

"Okay," replies Sienna, nodding her head up and down. The girl rises and slowly meanders away as Miss Carrie then turns her attention toward Isaac and Aubry. The two boys have been hovering around an empty mat, but they now are sitting criss-cross on the floor, waiting patiently for their turn with the teacher. From the bench, Miss Carrie leans toward them and explains, "You are going to do some sorting of short-vowel sounds." All three of them rise and make their way over to a shelf a few paces away. Miss Carrie selects two jars of materials and places one into Isaac's hands and another into Aubry's. "Now let's go sit down," she suggests, and they all return to the mat. Miss Carrie is on her knees, perpendicular to the two boys who sit along the long edge of the mat. Step by step, she explains the instructions, helps the pair arrange the materials properly, models how to do the activity, and watches them try a couple of practice runs. After about two minutes, Ella and Toby slowly make their way over, watching on the sidelines as Miss Carrie continues working with Isaac and Aubry. Within another minute, she wraps up and says, "I'm gonna leave you to do this and when you are all done sorting, you can get me." She smiles at the two boys for a moment. "Okay, so it's Aubry's turn, and then whose turn?" Isaac points at himself and Miss Carrie smiles broadly. "It's Isaac's turn. And then you go Aubry, Isaac, Aubry, Isaac, Aubry, Isaac— good?"

As the boys begin their work, Miss Carrie shifts her attention to Ella and Toby. The teacher walks on her knees to move over to their shared workspace on the floor—only a few feet from Aubry and Isaac's mat— and she collapses onto her hip to sit near them. "Okay. Let's see what this says."

Ella and Toby have laid out a set of wooden tiles on their mat. There are four columns to represent the place value of a four-digit number: the thousands, hundreds, tens, and ones. Miss Carrie points to the first wooden tile in the thousands column and Ella reads it. "One-thousand." One by one, Miss Carrie points to each number title in the column as Ella continues: "Two-thousand, three-thousand, four-thousand, five-thousand, six-thousand . . ."

"Wait a minute," interjects Miss Carrie, pointing again at the tile. "That's not a six-thousand." I glance over to look at the tile and it reads, in green printed numerals, *0006*.

"It's a nine!" exclaims Ella, reaching out, picking up, and rotating the tile, revealing it to be *9000*.

Toby then reaches for another tile a bit further down the column that reads *0009*, rotating it 180 degrees as he hands it to Miss Carrie. "This is a six!" he declares confidently.

Their teacher places the *6000* in its rightful place—below the *5000* tile—and Ella places the *9000* in the last space of the thousands column.

In light of these adjustments to their setup on the mat, I listen as Miss Carrie shares some advice with Ella and Toby, smiling as she talks. "You know what I've learned about math is that you have to be precise. So that means you have to, like, check your work. Make sure it's just right."

With that, Toby reaches for another tile in the tens column that looks like *08*, rotating it as he explains, "It was upside down." Together with Ella, the children fit it neatly in place.

As a follow-up, Miss Carrie continues her prior thought. "Checking your work and being precise. So now we check." She points back at the *6000*, now properly oriented, and together the three of them take turns reading each tile on the mat, one by one, to verify that they all are in the proper order and orientation. Once Miss Carrie sends Ella and Toby across the room to get the math manipulatives necessary for the next step of the work, she rises to her feet and touches base for a few moments with her teaching assistant, Miss Kristy, who also spends her morning circulating the room and checking in with individual children and pairs as they do their work.

Soon, Miss Carrie returns to her knees right next to Ella and Toby, to teach them how to do a place-value activity. I note that, from time to time, other children come check in with Miss Carrie for a few moments to make sure they are on track or to verify a next step in an activity they are working on—most often during a pause when Toby and Ella are away getting more materials for their lesson.

At one point, Miss Carrie turns her attention back to Isaac and Aubry. They have now finished sorting their cards, and Miss Carrie takes a couple of minutes to explain the directions for the next step—to use a set of cards with all letters of the alphabet to spell out each word adjacent to each picture card. "I'm just gonna solve the first one for you and you can go from there." Miss Carrie uses her fingers to "tap out" the word, finds the appropriate alphabet cards, and spells out the word on the mat, right next to the picture. She also tucks some of the picture cards back into their respective jars so that the two children have a more manageable task. After modeling the process, she says, "You all set to do this? You can work together," and promptly leaves the two boys on their own to collaboratively spell out the words.

Next, I watch as Miss Carrie toggles back to Ella and Toby, who have been waiting for her return so they can learn the next step of their math activity on place value. Miss Carrie first takes a quick walk around the room, at one point calling out to them, "I'm coming!" before rejoining them at their mat to go in-depth into the next segment of the lesson. After a few minutes of intense effort, as Ella and Toby are off gathering additional math materials for the next step of their work, she once again loops back with Isaac and Aubry on their vowel-sound matching and spelling using the letter cards. They have completed the first column of the work, spelling out six words with a short *o*. "So, let's check from the top," Miss Carrie suggests. Together, the three of them carefully review the list. A couple of words in, Miss Carrie draws their attention to a card with many dots on it and an arrow pointing just at a single point. "These are?" she inquires, pointing at the card. She quickly answers her own question. "Dots, right?" She then sounds out the word they have spelled, looking at the *d*, *o*, and *s* cards the boys placed on the mat. "Ddd-aaah-sss. Dos. Wait a minute!" she exclaims, sitting up tall on her knees.

"Dots," says Isaac.

"Oh. Did you hear that?" she asks. She then taps out each letter sound with the fingers on her right hand as she stretches out the word. "So, dddd-aahh-ttt-sss. But it's a dot; they're pointing to one dot of many dots." Miss Carrie pushes the *s* card an inch to the right, creating a blank space for the missing sound. "What sound is this?" she asks, pointing at the gap.

"*T*," identifies Isaac.

"That's right. Did you hear that? Dot. Dot, and then these are dots."

After Miss Carrie checks Isaac and Aubry's work for a full five minutes, she again leaves them on their own to spell out a second column of words and moves to help the next child.

This brief snapshot of Miss Carrie's interactions with these five students encapsulates less than twenty minutes of the school day, a small fraction of the open work time on this particular morning. Notably, throughout this time, the other nineteen children pretty much operate on their own, without a great deal of intervention or close observation by teachers. Miss Carrie continuously cycles through these short check-ins, teaching Ella and Toby the various steps in their place-value work, reviewing Isaac and Aubry's spellings, closely reading and discussing ways Sienna can improve her story. Miss Carrie is always on the move, circulating to help these and many other children nudge their projects forward until the work time is over. All the while, the buzz continues in the room—music, talking, sounds of movement. The constant motion of both children and teachers reflects sustained thinking, effort, and engagement in their work; their interactions afford them opportunities to discuss, correct, and advance learning from mistakes.

LIFE IN MISS CARRIE'S ROOM: CHILDREN'S HOUSE AND THE MONTESSORI PHILOSOPHY

I enter Carrie Smith's classroom during her eighth year of teaching at Nevins Elementary, a public Montessori school in a small urban district. The group of children she teaches is extremely diverse, reflecting a variety of racial/ethnic groups and world cultures, as well as a range of socioeconomic backgrounds. Prior to her job at Nevins, Miss Carrie taught five years in two other schools, for a total of thirteen years as a Montessori teacher thus far. She first learned about the philosophy during her teacher training in college and was immediately hooked. "In Montessori classrooms, kids could do real life things, and I loved that everything was really well planned out—every inch of everything was thought of—and they were always thinking of the child first and setting them up for success. I love the emphasis on keeping education independent." Thinking back, she reflects that once "I found Montessori . . . I just never looked back. I love it!"

The Montessori setting is quite different from a typical public school in numerous ways; one major distinction is that the children stay with the same teacher for three consecutive years. In "Children's House"—the Montessori-specific name for the early elementary classrooms—Miss Carrie works with young students between the ages of three and six, who spend three years with her in what is the equivalent of two years of preschool and one year of kindergarten. She usually has twenty-four children each year—eight 3-year-olds, eight 4-year-olds, and eight 5-year-olds. As the kindergarten children step up to the next classroom for grades 1–3, a new cohort of young preschoolers comes in. While the first-years take time to observe and internalize the workings of their new classroom, the returning students arrive on the first day of the school year with community norms, interactional dynamics, and learning routines already well established. Through active modeling and assisting, the second- and third-year children frequently and eagerly help their teacher shepherd the newest additions to the class into the Montessori way.

Miss Carrie says that in Children's House, "my job is to teach them all their subject areas and make sure that they are learning, adjusting, and being good little members of the world." She addresses a lot of foundational skills that she says most people "don't really remember being specifically taught," including helping her young pupils to do more for themselves. Miss Carrie explains that if children say, "'Oh, I can't tie my shoes,' I'm like, 'Oh, you can't yet,' getting them to change their mindset." She also carefully attends to each child's participation in the peer group and development of social skills. Because of the long stretch of time she has with them, she really gets to witness each child's academic and personal growth. "It's amazing to see kids who come in and they don't know their letters or numbers or how to make a friend, and then—all of a sudden—by their third year, they can read and write and they've got friends and confidence. I feel like a part of their village for those three years."

While Miss Carrie's Montessori classroom, on a surface level, shares a few common characteristics with the other public-school classrooms I visit (e.g., word wall, cubbies, small chairs and tables, shared story reading), the physical layout and her instructional approaches are particularly distinctive by comparison. There is an area with a large rug, but it is not brightly colored and segmented—it is grey and there are no assigned spots. Rather than teacher-led activities, Montessori classrooms employ a child-centered, individualized, open format of learning. Hence, very little is done in a whole group, with all children gathered together to do a single task. Instead, Miss Carrie's students have an extended, uninterrupted, independent work time for around three hours each morning. Her large room is segmented into smaller, aesthetically appealing areas through the intentional placement of rugs, shelves, and various child-sized pieces of furniture, forming many cozy sections where students can work. The shelves contain a wide array of materials purposefully organized and in reach of even the smallest child.

During the work time, children can select an activity from hundreds of "works"—clearly defined sets of self-correcting, Montessori-specific materials that can be used with particular, learned procedures—that they can do individually or with one other child. The works take a wide variety of forms but are typically contained in an easily portable basket, tray, or box. Materials for the works often include cards, blocks, beads, bowls, or other objects made specifically for Montessori lessons. Children also can arrange flowers, create art, prepare snacks, clean or scrub objects, and more. These and other "practical-life" works help build fine-motor skills and important noncognitive abilities applicable to navigating common, real-world activities. I observe that sometimes Miss Carrie introduces new works in a whole-class demo; at other times she invites older students to guide younger students through for the first time; or she might sit with a student and show them herself, step by step.

Children can select only one of the "works" at a time, and they are free to do it at any location in the room but must keep their materials confined to a mat or small table surface that clearly defines their temporary workspace. Notably, the children can continue with a selected work until they determine they are done; they are not forced to put everything away at an arbitrary end time based on an external schedule. Instead, at the close of each day, numerous mats are always laid haphazardly around the floor, each containing partially completed work and very neatly organized sets of materials, as well as handwritten name cards that indicate the child or children most recently using them. This affords a placeholder so that children can pause when school ends but then return to their tasks-in-progress during the next work time, teaching them to determine when their work is complete, by their own measure.

Miss Carrie's teaching demonstrates one of the central tenets of the Montessori philosophy: *freedom within boundaries.* She facilitates their independent-learning experiences through the purposeful presentation of materials, providing each child the latitude to choose from a large, but finite, number of options based on what most draws their interest. Unless children reach a checkpoint at the end of an activity or run into challenges they cannot troubleshoot, they work freely and at their own pace. Once engaged in a work, the child holds what Montessori calls the *control of error.* As Miss Carrie explains it, "a part of Montessori is that kids should be able to make mistakes and the materials are self-correcting." Miss Carrie expects the children to use the resources provided to review their own work along the way, identifying and correcting their mistakes without constantly seeking out adults for feedback, clarifications, and answers. This structure invites and encourages the children to "believe in themselves, that they can do things."

At the same time, Miss Carrie is very attuned to the needs and progress of each child in her class. Because the entire Montessori class of three- to six-year-old children operates fairly independently every single day, Miss Carrie devotes all of her time to check-in conversations, just-in-time assistance when students get stuck, and one-on-one lessons. She does this with the dedicated help of a full-time assistant teacher who, under Miss Carrie's direction, supports the logistical and instructional needs of the classroom. Generally speaking, this assistant teacher role is integral to Montessori communities; in my observations, Miss Kristy is a clear and highly valued contributor to learning in Miss Carrie's classroom. Miss Carrie closely tracks each student's progress in their work across subjects and seems to miraculously recall even the finest-grained details off the top of her head, like their developing story ideas and improvements over the course of the year. She spends a lot of her time sitting or kneeling on the floor, and also flits from one place to the next, spending five minutes here, one minute there, fifteen minutes elsewhere—all governed by the needs of the one or two children she is with at any given moment.

While "pull-out" activities with individuals and small groups are common in most kindergarten classrooms, the term "pull-out" does not have much meaning in the Montessori context, because the children have such limited time in the whole group. Each student engages with self-selected works that vary in content and pacing from those of surrounding peers. As such, virtually all interactions with the teacher are separate from everyone else. This is the case for the entire time of my observations of Miss Carrie's classroom, aside from gatherings on the rug during the morning meeting, end-of-day dismissal, storybook shared readings, and some targeted kindergarten handwriting lessons.

For the sake of learning, Miss Carrie diligently protects her one-on-one time with individual children and expects others to respect the boundaries of these interactions. On many occasions, I see her maintain laser-like focus on the child she is working with, even as students call out her name, or silently place a hand on her shoulder to indicate that they want to talk to her. Some students stand for a long time waiting for a turn; however, "I'm in the middle of a lesson" or "Ask three then me" are her common refrains when someone tries to interrupt her intensive work with another student. This reminds children of the class norm that they may not disrupt a peer's lesson, and that they should turn to the other resources in the class—their fellow learners—to get answers to questions before coming to a teacher. On rare occasions, I see her respond even more directly when children try to get her attention; in a gentle voice, she remarks "You don't need a teacher" or "I showed you how to do it, now you go do it." Within the Montessori context, as I understand it, these comments are an attempt to build independence, resilience, self-regulation, and problem solving, pushing the children to first turn to themselves for ideas about how to get back on track, rather than seeking external directives or affirmations from others.

Watching Miss Carrie enact the Montessori curriculum, I gather that her role in the class is that of a guide who remotely oversees each individual student's extended learning journey over the course of days, weeks, or months and is available as a support to the children on an as-needed basis. It is as if each child selects a single destination from numerous options—one of the Montessori "works"—and heads out on the highway for a lengthy road trip on their own or with a peer. During their journey, the children traverse well-established highways of Montessori activities and techniques. Although they cannot deviate from those preplanned pathways, the students can determine where and in what order they want to go to various destinations; they also have total control of the speed of the journey and when to pull over for a periodic rest stop. Miss Carrie's expectation is simply that they stay focused on moving forward, at their own pace and in their own way. She creates an environment in which the children learn to be self-reliant and to spend most of their time on their own, checking their maps and directions for themselves before touching base with the teacher. When they inevitably make wrong turns, stall their progress, or hit traffic slowdowns along the way—that is, mistakes, misunderstandings, confusions—the Montessori curriculum is self-correcting by design and the materials serve as a map to help children guide themselves back on track toward their destination, which they are able to do the bulk of the time. But if they really get turned around and cannot find a way to move forward, their faithful guide, Miss Carrie, is always no more than a quick call away, willing and able to help point them back to their planned route. Although she's always available and may provide tips and suggestions for how to get back on the highway, the children continuously remain in the driver's seat.

As a Montessorian *aid to life*, Miss Carrie offers guidance and support to the whole child. This means she holds in mind not only the various academic needs but also the development of a child's sense of self, emotions, and ability to interact with others in the community. While academic progress is important, Miss Carrie shares with me that her "major goals are for them to be happy at school, to follow the ground rules and the expectations, and be aware of others and thoughtful to them." With these aims, she hopes that "it's a happy, joyous place" for the children, and that they "buy in" to the classroom way of doing things. "I want them to walk in the door and want to be there" and for them "to share their selves with us." Miss Carrie wholeheartedly believes that making sure the children feel good in class is "the most important thing because when you have all that in place, I think you can learn anything."

RIDING SOLO: ENCOURAGING INDEPENDENCE AND SELF-CORRECTION

> It is surprising to notice that even from the earliest age, man finds the greatest satisfaction in feeling independent. The exalting feeling of being sufficient to oneself comes as a revelation.
> —Maria Montessori

Miss Carrie's Montessori teaching places children in the driver's seat of their own learning. Although she periodically interacts with each child here and there, her involvement is strategic and intermittent, rather than central to the flow of day-to-day activities in the classroom. Although the children cannot go "off-road" and deviate completely from the established way to use the materials, they do their works independently, advancing step-by-step to completion at their own speed and on their own nuanced path. When students get mixed up, she keeps her interventions to a minimum; instead, she leaves space and time for the children to make course corrections—double checking their planned route on the map, reversing their views, backing up, and heading a different direction on the highway—all on their own. I remember hearing Miss Carrie tell a couple of children engrossed in a work, "I'm gonna let you guys fix this one on your own. I'll scoot out of the way for you." This is what she does all day—get out of the children's way as they steer their self-directed learning and correct things for themselves.

One of the simplest manifestations of this approach comes in asking children to claim unlabeled pieces of student work. One day, prior to starting the day's work time, Miss Carrie addresses the class during a brief morning meeting with all children seated on the rug. "Before I say good morning, we found these beautiful paintings, but we don't know whose they are." This is a common mistake in her classroom—forgetting to put away work when finished and/or forgetting to put a name on the paper. She shares the attributes of the work to everyone, whether it is describing the image on a piece of art or reading a portion of writing. In the end, there is a natural consequence for the child who doesn't speak up because, as Miss Carrie puts it, "If we don't know whose it is, we put it in the recycling." I notice that she makes these announcements even if she likely does know the owner—for example, several kindergarteners she'd been working with lost some pages from the stories they have been writing. Rather than tell the children directly, she creates a space for them to figure it out for themselves—and they almost always do rise to the challenge.

On a related note, there is a norm that children should pick up after themselves when things get out of place. In the context of simple spills—which happen all of the time in Children's House—I note, time and again, that Miss Carrie has little to no reaction when children accidentally drop things. For the most part, she might just glance over for a moment and then continue with whatever she is doing, or calmly prompt the child to take action; for example, "You knocked the pencils over by accident. Just pick it up so we don't fall." I ask her about this in a follow-up interview and she explains that this is merely "cause and effect"—drops are a direct result of giving the children more independence. Although "a lot of kids will drop something and they kind of look at you for your reaction," Miss Carrie tells them "you just pick it up and just keep on going, like 'No big deal.'" In a nutshell, these natural mistakes are treated as nonevents, reflect the fact children are working on their own, and are easily corrected with minimal fanfare.

When it comes to more academic activities, Montessori works have the answers built right in so that after completing a task, the children can check for mistakes themselves. Cards used to sort letter sounds or rhyming words note the right groupings on the back side, so that children can easily flip the cards over after sorting them, to see whether they arranged them properly. Children often use the moveable alphabet—a set of letter cards or wooden shapes—that allows students to spell words and build sentences without producing written print; some works provide a tiny book with correct spellings for checking their answers after they have tried to sound out words on their own. When tracing wooden forms of continents or countries to create their own maps, the children can see that the pieces necessarily fit together like a puzzle and match the paper maps they use as a guide, making it obvious when a mistake has been made in orientation or labeling. To complete problems for math, children very frequently use "units"—or small beads—representing a count of one.

They can be carefully counted into groups of ten and exchanged for ten-bars—formed from ten beads fused together into a line—to represent place value during addition and subtraction problems; students can count and recount the beads and bars as many times as necessary using the tangible materials in front of them. In all of these cases, Miss Carrie—and the Montessori curriculum in general—believes children are able to discern for themselves whether they have properly completed a task. Subsequently, students can use the provided tools and learned processes to check and fix their work, even when the teacher is not watching.

However, sometimes this is a big ask for young children who are doing challenging work! Not surprisingly, they might be tempted to look at the answers right away before first attempting the work, thereby side-stepping the important experience of trial-and-error learning. On a few occasions, I see Miss Carrie gently remind children not to look until they try first.

- "The answer's there but we didn't do it yet, so I'm gonna flip those over."
- "We have to sort all these but it's tricky. We can't look at the back. Do you promise?"
- "Oh—you can't look, so let's put it down again."

The expectation is that, no matter the challenge, the children should keep pressing and not look up the answer until they complete their very best attempt on their own.

When children express uncertainty and turn to her for answers, Miss Carrie expresses confidence that they can complete the task. She then turns it back to the child, pushing for independent problem solving by saying something like, "You decide what you think is best," without telling them exactly what to do or which direction to go. When the children come to her with a question or something they find confusing, she usually provides hints or redirection, but promptly turns the control of the learning experience back over to the students as soon as they are all clear on directions and next steps. I hear this on several occasions at the end of clarifying check-ins with students:

- "I think you are ready to do this on your own, okay?"
- "I think you've got the hang of it. You think so? If you need help, just come get me."

- "Why don't you put all the pieces back? I'm sure you'll figure it out."

Notably, in many instances like this, Miss Carrie physically exits the interaction by standing and moving away from the workspace, leaving the child to continue to wrestle with the challenge independently.

Miss Carrie wants children to control the pace and the steps in the learning experience, so she often defers to their thinking, even while guiding them with subtle or not so subtle hints. If she intervenes too much at these times when they don't know exactly what to do, she would disrupt their learning. This would be akin to snatching the steering wheel out of the child's hands, usurping their control and autonomy over their journey toward the current learning destination. But if children are at a crossroads and truly do not know which way to turn, she does not leave them floundering; with gentle actions, she helps guide them back toward the highway so they can continue to progress toward their intended destination. For example, one morning, Ella comes over to ask for help to move a basket of books. Miss Carrie sits on the floor, flanked by two mats, as she helps Jack and Samuel with their respective works. When there is a pause in the flow of the work, she turns to Ella, who has quietly stood next to her for a few minutes, waiting to check in.

As Ella stands next to Miss Carrie, she rises only a head above her teacher who is seated criss-cross on the floor. Today Ella wears a bright blue T-shirt decorated with cartoon characters, a frilly pink ballet skirt, and matching pink stretch pants. Her brown hair is pulled back into a messy bun and her face is framed by short bangs that curve slightly, covering most of her forehead. Ella's eyes widen and she gestures wildly with her hands as she explains to Miss Carrie that she's having trouble with the basket. "I'm pushing it and it can't move."

"Oh my gosh," says Miss Carrie. "Remember what we learned about motion? That means you need more force." In this comment, she hearkens back to a science lesson she led with the children in the prior week. They went outside and used a swing to test out how to use force to move people and objects. With that guidance, Ella immediately saunters away.

Miss Carrie continues her work with Jack and Samuel. A couple of minutes later, Ella and two friends come over, collectively carrying a large, white, plastic laundry basket full of books and dropping it right next to their teacher.

When they do, Miss Carrie remarks, "Teamwork's the best work," and then spends the next minute or so looking in the basket to help Ella select some books for a research project she is working on.

When Ella first approaches her, Miss Carrie does not provide any help with the task of relocating the basket. Instead, she makes a connection to the class's recent science lesson about force and urges Ella to consider applying that knowledge to this real-world conundrum. Given her size, I think that most likely she physically could not have moved the books on her own. It would have been easy for Miss Carrie to just move the basket for her, but she leaves the troubleshooting to Ella, who very quickly crafts a plan to get the job done with the help of a couple of classmates who are willing to help. This is Miss Carrie's response when children get stuck on practical dilemmas like this, as well as more academic tasks that the children pursue.

When children come to check in with Miss Carrie for various academic projects, she first confirms that they have used the classroom resources to attempt to identify and self-correct mistakes. For example, before she even looks at newly written stories that the children present to her, I hear her verify that they already have checked their own writing using tools in the classroom.

On one occasion, I watch Sienna, Lucas, and Kamil come up and surround Miss Carrie with their writing work in hand, asking for her to review it. She is seated in a chair helping another child, and they stand behind her, waiting patiently for her to finish. When it is their turn to chat, she says, "Yes! Friends, hi!" in a bubbly voice, clasps her hands together, smiles broadly, and looks back and forth at the three children surrounding her. Sienna, who stands to Miss Carrie's right, speaks softly and quickly, her voice so quiet I cannot hear her words, even though I'm sitting just a few feet away. In response, Miss Carrie's first question, before even looking closely at their papers, is "All right, so did you do the proofreading list and the writer's checklist?" She looks straight at Sienna as she speaks; the girl remains quiet. With her tongue slightly sticking out of her mouth, Sienna shakes her head back and forth quickly, indicating she did not do this check.

"You remember the proofreading list is a page in your folder," she says to the three children, as she mimes the opening of a folder.

Lucas shakes his head yes.

"My proofreading list," repeats Miss Carrie. Lucas and Sienna walk away immediately. Kamil remains at the table, with a hand on Miss Carrie's shoulder. She continues her thought, talking to Sienna from a distance. "I think it's a great strategy to use because it helps you remember everything." She then turns to look at Kamil and asks, "Did you do your writer's checklist?" He indicates that he did, and she declares, "Great!" He sits next to her and she takes time to closely read Kamil's story and discuss it with him.

After the children do this checking process for themselves, Miss Carrie seems glad to go ahead and review their work. But attempts at self-assessment and self-correction are built in as a standard step of their writing process. Sometimes her reminders about self-evaluation address the quality of their work ("Is that your best work?"), whether they were careful and checked it ("Were all of these the right sounds? Did you check?"), and whether they are ready to move on to the next step, task, or activity ("There should be a check on every page. Is there?"). Rather than tell the children that they are wrong or are not done, she frames it as a question for them to determine for themselves.

In all of these cases, the onus for corrections is placed on the children. The support of process checklists, answer keys, and quick verbal reminders from the teacher empower children to check their own work. These tools work efficiently like a map, encouraging students to orient themselves and to determine how much further they have to go in the current leg of their journey, all with little to no intervention from Miss Carrie. Because of the norms and routines established in Miss Carrie's classroom, self-correction is possible for most students even without the constant, watchful gaze of a teacher over their shoulder.

MAPPING THE WAY FORWARD FROM MISTAKES: FEEDBACK THAT FOSTERS SELF-IMPROVEMENT

In her tone of voice, facial expressions, and words, Miss Carrie perpetually cheers and affirms the students as they pursue various academic and social challenges. When students get things right, she says, "I agree" or "Very good." When they get something right after a struggle, she praises their effort and expresses her confidence in their abilities. For example, during a one-on-one check-in after a long session with repeated mistakes and lots of teacher feedback, Lucas exchanges units for ten-bars correctly. "You did it! You're learning how to exchange!" she says with a smile, later noting, "I knew you could figure this out."

Miss Carrie's excitement swells as she reminds students of the enormous growth they have demonstrated during their time in her classroom. She compares past to present performance to accentuate just how far a child has journeyed over time. At one point during a one-on-one writing check-in, I watch as she excitedly shares with Aiden about the progress he has made with his writing since the beginning of the year.

They sit next to each other at a round table, and Aiden places his most recently written story on the surface between them. He starts to read, but before he can get far, Miss Carrie interrupts with a moment of excitement.

"Look at your writing! Holy smokes! Wait a minute. No, no, no—I have to show you this." Miss Carrie reaches across the table and opens his purple folder that contains pieces of writing that have been collected over many months. She starts leafing through pages, and Aiden joins in as they flip back through time, glancing over a great many stories that he has created. "Okay, let's look from the beginning of the year." She finds one book and pulls it out, opening to a page. "Look at your writing before. It's just like, not really on the lines. And now look at it." She points to his most recent piece of writing that they have been discussing. "Look! You used to use uppercase, now you use lots of—"

"—lowercase," offers Aiden.

"Wow!" exclaims Miss Carrie, smiling broadly with a joyful laugh. "Awesome!" She puts the book back in its place, closes the writing folder, and pushes it to the side so they can return their attention to Aiden's new story. "It's good to see what you learned, right? Sorry! I got excited."

Miss Carrie rests her cheek on her fist and turns her gaze back to Aiden's current work. I notice he has a slight smile on his face as he reads; as she listens, she smiles even harder. I can sense the joy she experiences in realizing just how far Aiden has come over the course of the school year. In moments like this, I am struck by the big-picture thinking that Miss Carrie displays and conveys to her students. She looks at learning and development in an arc over time, rather than solely focusing on the progress made during the most recent segment of the journey.

Even when praising students, Miss Carrie often embeds additional corrective feedback into her comments, throwing in a small area for improvement or an opportunity to extend the answer:

- "Great! Add your period."
- "Beautiful! June—today is the first day of June, so . . . what's the year?"

After years of serving as a guide for learning, Miss Carrie knows the highways of the Montessori landscape inside and out. She readily affirms children if they are on the right path. But, because of her wealth of knowledge in Montessori methods, she eagerly helps her students by also suggesting some of the local backroads and shortcuts—recommended, tried-and-true strategies and tactics that she knows can aid improvement. These can allow the child to refine the route and make for a better ride.

An example of this occurs on one particular morning as Miss Carrie engages in an exchange with Margaret as they review her spring-themed Writer's Workshop piece. Miss Carrie positively frames Margaret's work and also points out several mistakes that she could correct when editing.

Miss Carrie again sits at the round table as Margaret stands next to her; the girl's blonde, wavy hair falls on each side of her face, with a long braid sitting on her shoulder. There is an audience for their conversation. Aiden stands on Miss Carrie's other side; Samuel and Sienna are also sitting at the table—all working on their own projects or waiting for their turn to check in with Miss Carrie.

Miss Carrie fawns over the detail in Margaret's drawing; she and the four children look at the page. "Oh my gosh. You even remembered to do grass. You put a lot of details, you put a robin." Then suddenly she pauses, points at the illustration, and furrows her brow. "Wait a minute," Miss Carrie declares, with a note of skepticism in her voice. She turns toward Margaret and asks, "Does a robin have a mouth like us?"

On the page, Margaret has drawn the recognizable shape of a bird, but rather than sketching a beak, she has drawn a scooped line to make a smiley face.

Margaret quickly snaps her head away from the page and back toward her teacher. She breaks into a full smiley face, replete with squinted eyes, round rosy cheeks, and a slight giggling.

"Uh-oh," says Miss Carrie. "I'll hold on to this so you can check. I'm just gonna put what we call a little dog ear, so you know to come back to this one." She folds down the corner to mark the page. "Oopsah daisies—come back to this one." \

Miss Carrie turns through the balance of the pages, pointing out items here and there to check:

- "When you see grass—what color is grass?"
- "You're gonna color the tree trunk, right?"
- "Can I show you how to draw the leaves' veins, where they get their water from like this? . . . that's a beautiful detail."

Along the way, Miss Carrie conveys that Margaret has done good work but, through these comments, does not hesitate to intersperse corrective feedback, pointing out that she has forgotten some details and still needs to loop back to do "a few little checks" and make some revisions. Throughout, I note that the mood of the interaction between Margaret and Miss Carrie is jovial, marked by frequent smiles, eye contact, and shared laughter between the two of them, as they enjoy the good work she has done and also talk about how to correct the remaining areas for improvement.

As they wrap up their discussion, Miss Carrie asks Margaret, "Do you feel like you need to stop for today?"

"Yeah," says Margaret.

"Okay," agrees Miss Carrie. "You've done a lot, so let's save it." With that, Miss Carrie tucks away the writing piece until a later time.

In this interaction, Miss Carrie draws attention to the incredible detail that Margaret puts into her picture. By asking questions, she helps her student understand both the strengths of her work and the mistakes she made that diminished the accuracy of the fine details of her drawing. She does not say Margaret's work is wrong or inaccurate but, through their interaction, pushes the girl to rely on her own knowledge of robins and grass to reconsider her initial rendering.

Occasionally, when offering an explanation or redirecting a child to try again, I hear her refer to the need to be precise or accurate. At one point, I hear her say to the children, "Some things really have to be precise, and some things you try your best." Later, when I ask her about this language, she explains that this is not from Montessori; she learned it during a district-wide professional development training. She finds that she uses this terminology more in math and counting than other subjects; "There's a lot of things you can be more loosey-goosey with," but in math, "if someone's doing it really well, I will be like, 'Oh, I'm noticing you're precise. You're taking your time when counting it.'" This orientation toward work manifests in some of the teacher-student communication toward mistakes, with her being willing to confront them with their own mistakes and to redirect them.

There are, of course, times when children make a valiant effort on their own but still do not recognize they have made a mistake in their work or cannot identify areas for improvement. It is as if they have taken a wrong exit off the highway without even realizing it. At moments like these, Miss Carrie momentarily steps into the learning process to help guide the student back to autonomous learning—sometimes with a light touch and other times with a heavy hand. Just as she does with praise, she consistently maintains her even-keeled, positive affect during corrective feedback. Frequently, I hear Miss Carrie tell the children "no" or "I disagree" in a slightly sing-song voice, smiling broadly as she probes students for clarifications, additional details, and self-corrections.

- "I disagree. I count more than four beads."
- "No! Listen. . . . We need one more. Ready—1, 2, 3, 4, 5, 6, 7, 8 . . ."
- "You think this says ten tens? I disagree."

Her commentary is always in a warm, friendly tone of voice and embedded in the context of a conversation to help them course-correct and continue to navigate through a learning task.

When a child is confused and cannot provide an answer, Miss Carrie may give a hint or—under some circumstances—even just tell them the answer directly. She does this to help them decode words, recall terms, or remember information from prior conversations. A quick example of this comes up when Miss Carrie helps Samuel with his short-vowel sorting work. The task is for him to match cards with images to their appropriate middle-sound short vowels—either short *o* (e.g., mop) or short *a* (e.g., cat) in this activity. Doing the letter-sound practice requires him to accurately identify each picture.

Samuel is moving along in the game when he picks up a card with a bat on it and stretches out the sound. "Bbb—aaaaah—ttt." He places the card with a bat on it just below a picture of a pat of butter he previously placed in the column for a middle *a*. Then, he picks up the next card. It has a picture of a large cooking pot.

"Pan," he whispers to himself. Then, in a moment of uncertainty, he suddenly holds up the card to Miss Carrie and asks, "What is this?"

Miss Carrie looks over and offers a hint. "Hmmm—you cook food in it."

Samuel turns it back to himself, looks at it, and coughs in his arm. "Pan" he says.

"Pot," corrects Miss Carrie.

With that, Samuel immediately places the card in the middle-sound short *o* column, then continues to sort the balance of the picture cards in the unsorted pile on his own.

In this instance, there is no way that Samuel can complete the task at hand—sorting the various vowel sounds in the middle of the words—if he misidentifies the image. First, Miss Carrie provides a clue to help him try to figure it out for himself; but when Samuel is not successful, she is willing to provide the answer. The point of the work is not picture iden- tification or labeling, but short-vowel matching, so she is quick to tell him the word so that he can demonstrate his understanding of the letter sounds. Similarly, a driver who senses they have taken a wrong turn might not be able to get back on the proper route without consulting a map or seeking a little guidance from a knowledgeable local. Although it is not her predominant way of supporting students, Miss Carrie uses this mistake response throughout my time in her class—a hint, followed by giving the children the quick answer—for a number of students in circumstances like this, where they simply cannot recall the information or decode the word. I see how this allows the activity to progress forward and focus on the learning at hand.

In contrast to the prior instances of pressing through the mistake to correct it, there are some occasions when the task is just too much and, even with dedicated engagement, Miss Carrie does not feel that the child has the background knowledge necessary to complete it independently. In these cases, she allows the student to truncate their time with the activity and offers advice on what other foundational skills are needed in advance of the task. It is as if she urges the child to pick a closer destination before setting out for a longer, more involved journey. An example occurs one morning as Zach and Isaac are working on a money work that includes an assortment of items labeled with prices. The children are supposed to match the coins to the proper amounts on the labels, then add together the costs of multiple items.

Miss Carrie touches base with the pair, asking Zach about the amounts they have assigned for each item they are pretending to buy during the game. The two children are sitting on either side of the front of their mat, and Miss Carrie sits comfortably on her knees next to Zach. As she begins checking in with the boys, she asks Zach to identify the coins, using three different questions: "What did you choose to pay with?" "What kind of coins did you use?" and "What are these called?"

After a couple of misunderstandings with the question, eventually Zach softly says, "Pennies."

"Pennies!" she exclaims. "So, you used six pennies. What could you use that has five cents?"

Zach looks down at the work but remains silent.

"Do you know which one is worth five cents?" Miss Carrie asks Zach again. Isaac reaches out his hand from the other side of the mat, full of nickels, but Miss Carrie waves him back for the time being and keeps the question directed toward Zach. He is still silent; Miss Carrie taps him lightly on the arm to get his attention. "Do you know which one is five cents?" she repeats, asking the question for a third time.

Zach's eyes scan the mat, and he points at one of the coins, talking softly in response to her question.

She asks yet again: "Do you know what it's called?"

Zach curtly says, "No," with a straight face.

"It's a nickel!" Miss Carrie says in a sweet voice, picking up the coin and holding it near him so that he can take a look. She continues, "A nickel is five cents. So, if you had a nickel, how much more would you have to add to make six?"

"Uh." He pauses briefly before confidently exclaiming, "One!"

"Yes!" Miss Carrie squeals, pointing at the two types of coins as she continues to explain. "Because the penny is one and the nickel is five," she explains in a lilting, pleasant voice. Miss Carrie pauses for a moment and points at the work before sharing an idea with Zach. "You know what I think maybe you could do before this is to do a money sort to figure out what everything is first." She turns and points to the shelf behind her, toward where that work is. "So, let's clean this up and go sort first, so you'll learn."

In order to do a work in which you add coins together, you need to first be able to confidently identify the name and value of each coin. When Zach seems unsure of which coin is a penny and which is a nickel, Miss Carrie offers the suggestion to go back a step and get some practice with coin recognition before looping back to try this work again later. She helps him figure out a more appropriate sequence in which to do the work—first do coin recognition, then once he arrives there, he can move on to adding together money values—so that he can have a successful learning experience at each step along the road.

EN ROUTE TO ANSWERS: USING DIRECT CORRECTIONS TO REDIRECT LEARNING

Because the children work independently most of the time, Miss Carrie often does not see their works until they are completely done. The Montessori materials serve as the children's map to their learning destination; they use the class resources to plan their route and to cruise the highways independently. Once they feel they have arrived at an interim or final destination, they have a chance to connect with their guide to touch base about how the journey is going. If the children confidently convey to her that they have earnestly attempted and thoroughly completed the works on their own, Miss Carrie does not hesitate to coach the children through revision, including crossing-out, cutting, or reordering words and images or, for smaller mistakes, using "accident tape"—white labels—to cover a mixed-up word or wrong letter that needs rewriting. These are more direct ways of pivoting the children's trajectories; corrective feedback and redirection allow for them to course-correct and get their learning back on track when they have made mistakes.

A small example of this arises when Kaia checks in with Miss Carrie about her most recent book in Writer's Workshop. Kaia has written a story about her experience sticking with different challenges, even when learning is hard. Miss Carrie points out that one of her sentences starts with the word "And."

Miss Carrie sits criss-cross on the floor with Kaia, flipping through a few pages of the book together. Kaia's dark brown hair is in a bob cut, and she is clothed in her summery pink dress with thin blue stripes as she stands next to Miss Carrie, fiddling her hands with the purple, plastic heart necklace she is wearing. Kaia watches Miss Carrie as she reads back her story aloud. When Miss Carrie gets to a page that reads, "And I didn't give up on the moveable alphabet," she suddenly looks up at Kaia's face and offers some feedback. "I have a question about this. Why are you starting with *And*?"

"I just really want it to start with *And*," insists Kaia.

"When you are making a list, you can start with *And*," explains Miss Carrie. "But ordinarily, you don't start a sentence with it." Miss Carrie asks Kaia to grab a marker from a nearby shelf. Kaia quickly gets one and then crouches down beside Miss Carrie, opens the black marker, and tries to cross out the word *And*. Miss Carrie takes the marker from her hand and retraces Kaia's *X* over the word *And*. She then reads back the result to Kaia: "I didn't give up on the moveable alphabet. See how it still flows." Miss Carrie goes back and rereads the newly edited page: "I didn't give up on the cubing chain. I didn't give up on the moveable alphabet." She looks at Kaia, who is gazing at her teacher with her chin resting in her hands. "Pretty good, right?" asks Miss Carrie as she turns the page.

Kaia remains crouched down next to Miss Carrie as the pair continue through the book, taking turns reading each page and using the black marker to make a few additional edits along the way. On the final page, Kaia again has included an *And*. "Do we need *And*?" Miss Carrie asks. Kaia gently shakes her head left and right, her chin cupped in her hands. "Noooo," says Miss Carrie, vocalizing Kaia's answer as she again uses the black marker to cross out the word *And* with an *X*. When they are done with their edits, Miss Carrie extends an offer to Kaia: "Do you want to read Miss Sara your story? Miss Sara would LOVE to hear it. Get the hall pass and ask for Miss Sara, our principal."

While she cheers Kaia's work on this book, she also emphasizes the writing rule of thumb that she wants her to apply for this and other projects: do not start sentences with the word *And*. Furthermore, Miss Carrie expresses pride in what Kaia creates, sending her to share the story with the school principal. Kaia does the bulk of her writing work correctly and independently; she only requires minimal guidance from Miss Carrie at the end to make the final corrections on her writing piece.

Beyond marking mistakes on student work, Miss Carrie does not hesitate to grab a nearby pair of scissors to cut and to reorder their papers if she feels it is warranted. For example, one day Malcolm does a work where he is supposed to answer the question "What are the seasons?" and write the words on the page in the correct order. However, on his paper he writes *Sumr*, *Srin*, *Fol*, and *Wtr*—making an admirable effort sounding out the words, but mistakenly switching the position of spring and summer in the sequence.

Because he has some seasons out of order, Miss Carrie invites Malcolm to reengage with his completed paper, an artifact of his independent thinking and efforts. Malcolm is a small, soft-spoken boy, and his thick, black hair is braided into cornrows and long braids that stretch down to his shoulders. During my time in her room, I observe that Miss Carrie interacts with him relatively often to give him academic support so he can complete his works. After an initial shared look at the paper as Malcolm reads each word, Miss Carrie says, "Okay, now we can put them in order. So . . . I'm gonna get scissors." Malcolm is standing there for a few moments before Miss Carrie asks, "Can you get the tape?" and he obliges.

A minute or so later, they reconvene with the materials in hand. Miss Carrie sits down and starts. "So, let's see. What season are we in now?" Miss Carrie scoots Malcolm's chair over closer to hers, presumably so they can both see the artifact well. Then, she looks up and steps outside of her moment with Malcolm to smile and say to me, "Oh, this is a good example." I take this as an indication that this is a mistake that she is about to help him correct.

"Spring," answers Malcolm.

Miss Carrie turns her attention away from me and back into the moment with Malcolm. "We're in spring. So, after spring, what will happen? Will the weather get chilly to fall?"

"No," says Malcolm, matter-of-factly.

Miss Carrie probes further: "Will it get hot for summer or cold like winter for snow?"

"Hot like summer," says Malcolm, choosing the right answer of the choices.

"Right," says Miss Carrie, looking intently at his page, with the seasons in the mixed-up order. "So, let's see. Hmm. What should we do . . . so, do you want to start with the season we're in now?"

Malcolm nods.

"So, what season are we in now?" asks Miss Carrie, urging Malcolm to recall his prior response.

"Spring," he reiterates.

"So, what I'm gonna do is I'm gonna cut this up," she says as she starts cutting around the box for each season, "and then we're gonna put the puzzle back in the right order." I watch as Miss Carrie guides him through placing the squares in order, and they use tape to reassemble the pieces correctly.

As I reflect on the exchange, it seems that Miss Carrie focuses on making sure Malcolm knows the seasons, and she is willing to sit with him and go back and forth until he can generate the responses for himself. Later, when I ask her about this particular exchange, she explains that Malcolm has documented challenges sustaining focus and, in the moment, she anticipated that asking him to cut it for himself would take an extraordinarily long time, longer than other children in the class. So, upon realizing his mistake, "In my mind, I thought . . . what is my intention? My intention was for him to do comprehension and to do writing." Thus, she does not ask him to cut and reorder the panels, which is a tangent to the main task of interest. Instead, she pulls out the scissors and cuts it herself to help preserve the good sounding out, letter printing, and illustrations Malcolm already has done for this task. At the same time, she still prompts him to redo the step of ordering the seasons and to tape the panels back together so that he can correct his initial mistake. Miss Carrie decides to be more heavy-handed in her corrections here in order to ensure that Malcolm can appropriately replot his route on the map and make his way back to the correct answer. While in this case the answer is clear-cut, she also frequently pulls out scissors whenever students write, and she wishes for them to make corrections or edits. In many of these cases, the drawings the students have made work well, but there are tweaks and adjustments she wants them to make in their writing—whether it is adding or taking out words or facts, clarifying confusing sentences, or rewriting with neater penmanship.

There are moments in which I watch Miss Carrie invite a child to take a guess, whether it is making an estimate in a math work or asking children if they have a hypothesis during a science demonstration. However, more often than not, this is not the goal of the works in the class; Miss Carrie explains that when the students are working, "sometimes you guess and sometimes you don't." If a child is offering a string of guesses, she might say, "Wait a minute, don't guess. Let's think," nudging them to rely on previously learned skills or steps. As their guide, she urges them to pull over to the side of the highway and reevaluate before moving forward. Before continuing their journey, Miss Carrie wants her students to consult their map—that is, instructions, materials, and so on—so they can properly navigate each learning experience, carefully following along the preplanned route to their destination rather than haphazardly guessing which way to go.

This comes up one day when working with Zach as he reads a book about squirrels. He is a tall boy in the class, with short brown hair and a gentle countenance. The pair sit huddled side by side at a small desk facing a large window in the class, so sunlight pours over the duo as Zach reads to Miss Carrie. Zach makes several mistakes along the way because he is guessing some of the words rather than decoding them—reading *it's* as *it is*, and *mother* as *mommy*. Miss Carrie gently corrects him each time, asking him to look closely and try it again, and repositioning his pointer finger so that he will track each word as he goes. Six minutes into this particular shared-reading session, Zach leans his arm onto his chin, momentarily propping up his head, and then pushes the palms of his hands into his face to rub his eyes. Through his body language, I can tell that he is starting to get fatigued by the lengthy and effortful session.

At that moment, Miss Carrie offers a pause for encouragement. "Okay," she says. "Let's take a deep breath . . . stretch out." She reaches her hands up in the air, and Zach follows her lead. The pair take a quick stretch break together. "Ahh," sighs Miss Carrie, launching a gentle entrée back into the task at hand. "What you wanna do is you want to read what the words say. Sometimes I do this, too; I have kind of a guess of what the words are." She pats the book as she continues to explain. "But you really want to read what the words say. So, let's try again." Zach yawns as Miss Carrie points to the top of the page, then cheerfully reads the first two words: "It's spring!"

"It's spring," repeats Zach, before continuing to the next part of the sentence. "A mother squirrel builds a nest." He is quickly stuck again, trying to figure out the next phrase in the sentence.

After a pause, Miss Carrie asks Zach, "What's a strategy we use if we don't know a word?"

"We can sound it out," he offers, looking up at Miss Carrie.

"Um-hmm," affirms Miss Carrie with a nod.

Zach turns around to the word wall behind him and mutters, "Sight word."

"No," says Miss Carrie, subtly shaking her head left and right. She points to the book. "Look at the picture!" she says eagerly, pointing at the page. "So, 'It's spring, a mother squirrel builds a nest in a—'" She stops abruptly at the cliff-hanger, placing her finger on her lips in a pensive pause. "Hmm."

After a pause, Zach breaks in with the next phrase. "Tree. In a tree."

"That's right," confirms Miss Carrie, before they continue to the next page.

In this example, Miss Carrie offers support to Zach as he pushes through reading a book that is very challenging for him. Despite the substantial length of time that it takes—twenty-five minutes in total—she sticks with him as he makes it through and does not let him opt out of the discussion, even as he is unsure of his answers. She conveys the expectation that Zach attend to the words on the page and avoid guessing when reading, reminding him that "you really want to read what the words say" and that they can use a strategy "if we don't know a word."

In each of these instances, Miss Carrie's intervention gives her student a do-over: an opportunity to sit with her, look at the map, and course-correct together. She steps in to reinforce a point, to clarify a confusion, and to make clear—verbally and in writing—what should be done next, all while supporting the child as they rectify the mistake and learn how to improve their work. Because she feels mistakes are "teachable moments" but dislikes when "mistakes go into reprimand," Miss Carrie sustains positive affect throughout mistake-related interactions. Whether it is tracking a child's reading, checking a mat arrangement, counting, adding or subtracting numbers, or identifying continents, Miss Carrie frames mistakes as a starting point for learning. When mistakes occur, she engages deeply with the child, asking questions to help elongate student responses and slowly reshape confusion into correct answers. From that point, the child can continue traveling down the road with Miss Carrie's guidance in mind, finishing up works independently, while continuing to steer their own learning process.

MAKING FOR A SMOOTH JOURNEY: BEHAVIOR
MANAGEMENT AND FOSTERING KINDNESS

While the core of the work in Miss Carrie's class is academic, I watch her prioritize social and behavioral norms in her interactions with the children. In order to do the academic work, she holds them to high standards for their behavior—how they interact with her, how they treat their peers, and how they attend to their work. When students do not meet her expectations, her responses are typically calm and polite, but firm and definitive:

- "If you have a question, you raise your hand. I'm not going to answer you when you're yelling, okay? I'm being very clear with you."
- "Friends, I want you to stop, look, and listen. Stop. Stop means 'Don't move.' Stop means 'Don't move.' And then look, which means you should see me. And then turn your listening on."

In these and other moments with the children, she reestablishes the norms she wants the students to adhere to so that they treat her and each other with respect, sometimes even firmly reminding them that "it's a learning time" to try to get them to self-adjust.

Miss Carrie's most stern reprimands go to how the students use materials, drawing their attention to potential damage. When Kaia repeatedly clanks some of the ten-bars against each other, Miss Carrie raises her hand in a stop signal and says, "Please don't destroy our materials." Or, when Isaac is not paying close attention when using the inkpad during the stamp game, she tells him, "You are putting the stamp on the mat and destroying the mat." In both cases, her very direct feedback conveys that they must stop what they are doing in order to take good care of the Montessori materials, using the word "destroy" to characterize the children's careless use of the items. I understand why this might be warranted, as there are a great number of materials in each classroom that are used year after year and—with a replacement value of tens of thousands of dollars per room—they are extremely expensive.

Further, when it comes to keeping workspaces tidy and using manipulatives properly, she is firm with the children, providing a lot of feedback on how to keep the room and their work well organized. She frequently reminds the children to tidy up mats and manipulatives, taking care to check that all items are on the mat; "I spy this beautiful bank game for Isaac and Aubry, but you need to make sure all of your work goes on the mat. Isaac and Aubry. Right?"

Miss Carrie also offers feedback about their listening skills, to make sure that people are quiet when she or someone else speaks. If students are not paying attention to the instructions, she gives them reminders: "I'll wait. I can't talk when everyone's speaking" or "I'll wait until everyone's hands are in their laps." Rudeness is not tolerated; she expects the children to "speak kindly" to her and to each other, and to use an appropriate tone of voice—for example, "I'm choosing not to answer because you're just yelling out at me." She guides these behaviors with a firm hand and does not allow for "road rage" if the children's emotions surge or they become cross; the expectation is that they will follow the established traffic etiquette and will be nice to each other as they are navigating their learning journeys. To foster positive interactions, Miss Carrie often provides the children with model language of how she would like them to respond, asking whether they will say "'Yes, please' or 'No, thank you'" and also calls the class's attention to peers who are modeling good behavior—for example, "Thanks for all the kids that are sitting criss-cross so nice."

Additionally, when children distract each other, Miss Carrie gives them polite but firm language to use in response. When Marie is talking to Cosette while Kaia reads the morning message, Miss Carrie interjects. "Cosette, will you be able to hear the message if Marie's talking to you? So, say 'I can't talk now!'" Or, when Mia is repeatedly tapping Kamil and he gets agitated, Miss Carrie asks, "Excuse me, Kamil. Instead of yelling at a younger friend, could you please speak to her nicely of what you don't want her to do? Because yelling at her is not a choice."

Kamil immediately turns to Mia and says, "Stop touching me."

Miss Carrie offers a correction in Kamil's harsh tone. She tells him, "Say, 'I don't want you to touch me, please,'" modeling a gentler tone.

"I don't want you to touch me, please," echoes Kamil.

Miss Carrie leans toward the two children and reinforces the point with Mia. "Do you hear that, Mia? He's saying he doesn't want you to touch him. Okay?"

Then, the teacher reiterates the point to Kamil. "Please speak kindly to us."

Miss Carrie's modeling allows her to scaffold the interpersonal interaction between Kamil and Mia. She gives Kamil the model language and the green light to communicate respectfully to his peer—despite being annoyed with her actions—and ensures that Mia knows how to change her behavior to be more respectful. This social support is a regular occurrence in Miss Carrie's classroom; I see it every day I am in the class.

In the moments when students do not meet the group norms, she extends opportunities for children to self-assess and consider their actions. When emotions run hot and children may be visibly upset, crying, or raising their voice, Miss Carrie has a "peace corner" and a "calm-down stool" in her room—designated spots where children can pause for a while to gather themselves before reengaging in their prior activity. She positions these spaces as potential getaways where a child can elect to take time to regroup rather than as forced timeout areas to separate them from others. I observe that most of the children interact with them as tools rather than as punishments.

In Miss Carrie's classroom, student behavior commonly links to academics through her expectation that children will stay focused on their work. One way she helps encourage students to focus on the speaker when in a group is to call out the specific names of students who talk over their peers or yell out without raising their hands and waiting to be called. "When you yell out an answer, it's hard for someone to think. . . . We really want to stick with raising our hands. Okay?" With attention to this aspect of classroom discourse, she protects the think time of other children who might not land on an answer so quickly and can benefit from time to process the question at hand. It also means that she expects them to pay careful attention to directions when they are being given, to ensure that they know what they need to do when they are working on their own. Whether working with an individual or addressing a group, Miss Carrie will sometimes ask students to repeat back the directions, saying things like, "Can someone help us name what we learned from the message?" or "Think of two things you learned. Look at your chart and it will help you." This pushes the responsibility back onto the children to track the information given to them and to be able to repeat it to her and others.

When children are doing their works, they are expected to make consistent, daily progress, advancing through each segment of their learning road trip at a good pace. In my observations, I notice that another behavioral mistake that seems to commonly precipitate a big response from

Miss Carrie is when students are off task. Because each individual child's work is not closely monitored by their teacher at every moment, they must manage themselves. Although this is a challenge for young students, the majority—after months of practice over the course of the school year—do appear to stay on task for most of the work time. However, there are times here and there throughout each day when someone does not maintain focus, and Miss Carrie gives a clear, firm, and quick reminder.

- "Isaac, please do work."
- "I'm confused because you've been working on this all morning, but you haven't gotten anything done."

Without clear expectations, I can only imagine where this free-flowing, self-guided, three-hour block could go. If Miss Carrie did not have norms, practice with the materials, and expectations about self-management, it could be complete chaos.

From my perch in the classroom, I watch Miss Carrie's extreme patience with children as they take hours or even multiple days to complete tasks; but she wants to be sure that they are consistently edging forward along the road to success. More importantly, she demands that they complete each task that they take on. Numerous times I see her check in with the children to ensure that if "you started your work, you finished your work." If they do not finish, she sends them back; they cannot move on to the next activity until the prior one is completed and checked by their teacher. Then, they also must completely clean up their mat or work area before they can select and start on their next work.

Built into Miss Carrie's assessment of whether they are working at a good pace and finishing their works is her expectation for the children to do the best work that they can. This comes up often, whether she is affirming children for what they have completed ("When you two really focus, you can get work done. You're getting it done quickly but you're doing it right. You're trying your best, right?"), nudging along children who are not entirely on task ("I know both of you, you need to be turning your best thinking on."), or gently reprimanding a child who has gotten lost in the process of a work activity ("We're doing this so you can learn it so you'll know how to do it next year. So, you have to really try.").

Whether honing listening skills, modeling communication tactics, or offering reminders to give their work all they've got, Miss Carrie devotes a fair amount of attention to children's behaviors. She helps correct their actions so that they learn to be more respectful and focused in her classroom.

LEADING BY EXAMPLE: MODELING ADAPTIVE REACTIONS TO MISTAKES

The children have a great deal of awareness about mistakes, which comes across brilliantly during one particular morning meeting in the classroom. Once settled in a large ring around the border of the classroom rug, Miss Carrie shares with the children, "Miss Maleka is interested in mistakes." She then asks, "What do you know about mistakes?" In response, several children raise their hands and, one after the other, the young students take turns answering and sharing their perspectives.

- "If you make mistakes, you can try again and again." —Ella
- "If you feel mad, go to the peace corner and do calming breaths." —Sienna
- "If you make mistakes, it's good. . . . I was told that. I don't know why." —Margaret
- "It's good to make mistakes because you learn." —J.T.
- "When you make a mistake, it grows your brain." —Kamil
- "When you make a mistake, your brain gets smart." —Malcolm
- "When you make a mistake and feel you can't get it, just try and try and try and you'll get it." —Isaac
- "If you make a mistake, you can talk about it and calm down." —Louis

In listening to the students, it seems apparent that they have talked about this topic before. Immediately, I am struck by how articulate these young children are when demonstrating—in abstract terms, no less—the importance of mistakes to their learning. Also, I note that their responses are incredibly adaptive and "growth-mindset" oriented, recognizing the emotional components of mistakes—while still positioning them as opportunities—and highlighting the importance of trying again.

When children make mistakes and don't know how to resolve them or when they express a lack of confidence in their work, Miss Carrie volleys back with gentle encouragement. When Gabriella stays silent when asked whether she knows what a character in a book is, Miss Carrie deduces that she does not have an answer. "You don't know?" she asks. "You don't know yet! I'm gonna help you." She then goes about building an answer for this with the involvement of other students. A moment of encouragement like this also comes about when Samuel needs to draw a picture of a kite in his Writer's Workshop story, and he briefly checks in with Miss Carrie about it.

While sitting with Miss Carrie and Sienna, Samuel readily admits that he does not know how to draw a kite. Miss Carrie asks him, "Do you know how to draw a diamond?" and encourages him to "ask a friend— Sienna knows." But even after Sienna demonstrates how to do it, he does not know what to do with what he has already drawn, which looks a little like a lollypop on a stick rather than a kite on a string.

"I have to draw it again. I have to draw it again." Samuel has a note of worry in his voice. He seems mildly distressed that he has not quite gotten this right.

"Go for it. Do it," Miss Carrie says encouragingly.

Samuel starts to explain, "I have to scribble all of . . ." He trails off, looking down at his current shape on the page.

Miss Carrie gently suggests, "Can't you just do, like, a diamond around it?"

"Yeah, that's what I did," says Samuel.

Miss Carrie further elaborates her advice to Samuel. "'Cause when you make a mistake, you just, like, try to figure out how to make it into something else."

In response to Samuel's frustration, Miss Carrie urges him to be more flexible in his approach to correction. Rather than start over from scratch or "scribble all of" it, she suggests that he create a new thing out of his mistake. In this and at other moments, Miss Carrie is always looking for the bright side and the way forward. She does not want children to abandon their destination when things do not go as expected; instead, she hopes they will find an alternative route that allows them to continue down the highway.

In addition to encouraging students, she also has no hesitation in admitting her own mistakes and struggles. I see this happen a lot, and she actually makes a big fuss about it with the children, and models adaptive strategies when she makes mistakes in front of them. One time she is modeling a work in the practical-life area of the room. Here, children can zip, button, pour liquids, use pretend cookware, and also pretend to care for a baby. On this day, Miss Carrie demonstrates how to bathe a baby doll and change its clothing—a new work that she has recently put out and that the children will be able to choose during the morning work time.

As the entire class watches, Miss Carrie puts on a smock, puts some water in a basin so that she can wash the small doll, washes it with a couple of pumps of water on a wet washcloth, dries it, and puts on a play diaper. I observe that its tiny, brown body is surprisingly realistic. As she starts to put the clothes back on the baby, she offers a warning to the children. "Sometimes these outfits are a little tricky to put on, so you know what I like to do? Put the legs in first." She easily puts the doll's legs in but then asks, "What next?"

A child suggests that she should try the arms. "The arms I find are a little bit tricky. Kind of have to . . . push them through a little." She gives it a go, continually adjusting the doll as she tries to get the arms in, but she really struggles to put the tiny clothes on.

From the throng of children huddled around this demonstration, someone quickly adds, "You could also ask a friend."

"Oh," replies Miss Carrie. "Like, if I couldn't do it, I could ask a friend?"

"Yes."

"Yeah, I could," concedes Miss Carrie. She pauses for a couple of seconds, inspecting her work to try to find a way through. She keeps turning and pushing to try to get the arm through. "Oh, this is very tricky but I'm not going to give up. Just gonna keep trying different ways. Oh, I see, if I wiggle it up. Oh, baby."

Here, Miss Carrie demonstrates that the children will likely hit speed bumps—or even roadblocks—that stall their progress toward finishing this work. She is transparent about how these obstacles will probably delay everyone, even an experienced guide. When Miss Carrie is upfront about the fact that she herself finds a task difficult, it reinforces the point that the children will likely have to stick with it for a while to be successful. Sharing this insight in advance can help them mentally prepare for when slowdowns happen in their own journeys. When a child suggests that she ask a friend for help, Miss Carrie acknowledges that is a possibility but still presses on, modeling the stick-to-it approach that they may need to help them finish navigating the task on their own. The point of a work like this is to go through the process; just finding someone to put the clothing on the baby for them diminishes the opportunity for children to perform the practical-life skill.

Admitting mistakes comes up in academic tasks, as well. When reading a book on butterflies, she asks her teaching assistant and me to remind her how to pronounce the word *pupae*, admitting out loud—in front of the whole class—"I'm having a hard time with that word but I'm not going to give up." After clarifying the answer with Miss Kristy, Miss Carrie offers a takeaway for the children: "Sometimes you just have to ask a friend. I needed help from a friend." On another occasion while working with Toby on writing out words that start with *v*, she says, "I am always forgetting how to spell the word *vacuum*. I'm going to look it up. I never remember if it's two *u*'s or two *c*'s." This is a common mistake for adults, let alone young children. This signals to Toby that this is a challenging word and puts teacher and child in the same boat when it comes to this.

Sometimes Miss Carrie's mistakes have to do with simple errors or forgetfulness. One morning the classroom phone rings and when she answers, it is the music teacher asking for her kindergarten students to come down for their class.

Miss Carrie claps to get the class's attention. "Kindergarteners, I'm so sorry, we forgot to put our timer on for music. So, we need to line you up. On the count of three, all the K's have to be lined up, okay? I'm sorry that we forgot to put our timer on."

She continues to apologize as the children quickly tidy their work and line up to go to the class that has already begun with kindergarteners from all of the other Children's House classrooms in the school. "Friends, you gotta walk quickly, carefully, as fast as you can. Go in so quiet, I'm so sorry."

Once Miss Kristy leads the group out the door and down the hallway to the music class, Miss Carrie looks down at Rupal, a small girl in her first year in the classroom. Miss Carrie shakes her head left and right with a somewhat sad face as she quietly admits to her, "I have the hardest time with that, Rupal."

In this example, Miss Carrie not only takes full personal responsibility for the mistake, she also shows vulnerability in saying this is something that she has a hard time with and is trying to work on. She models that she is also on a journey of her own; in this and other instances, when Miss Carrie takes a wrong turn in front of everyone, she does not shy away from admitting her mistakes, big or small.

In these moments, Miss Carrie's own mistakes flow right into the motion of the class. She does not try to hide them; she does not push them onto the students or the class as a whole. She is transparent about her mistakes and efforts to figure out her next steps to resolve them—whether it is to erase and correct her writing, to seek help from a student or fellow teacher to figure it out, or to acknowledge that she needs to keep practicing something so she can improve.

ANTICIPATING NEW ADVENTURES AHEAD

> We wanna build them up, we don't wanna tear them down. . . . Look at the mistake and think, "What could I do to help them?" . . . Really look at each child, and think, "What can I do to help them understand?" . . . And just be mindful of how you speak to a child, just as you would an adult.
> – Miss Carrie

Throughout my time in Room 132, I watch Miss Carrie set children loose to drive themselves on their own chosen pathways to learning. Miss Carrie's teaching approach—anchored in her many years of Montessori training and experience—simultaneously provides strong scaffolding and consistent guidance to the children, while also keeping the onus on them to select the fine-grained details of their daily learning experience. Each student is free to chart their own course and hit the road; the children decide what to work on, where to set up their materials, and who to work with. When done, they check their own answers. In doing so, Miss Carrie empowers her young pupils to truly control how they navigate the bulk of their day.

The pace of learning in her classroom is slow, by design. By the time a child sits with Miss Carrie, they have typically already spent hours or even days independently working on a task. Her aim is to "create a safety net" in which the children can receive just-in-time support from her when needed for their independent learning. Embracing her belief that "mistakes are a part of life," Miss Carrie is purposefully gentle with her words, talking to the children in a manner that reflects how she "wants to be treated."

At the same time, she very clearly and kindly conveys that she will not complete or fix their works for them. This is no joyride; the children absolutely must do things for themselves. They are on a planned road trip with a destination that will take weeks, months, or years to reach. With each work they advance toward a particular interim destination, and each mile of the journey affords opportunities to practice and build fluency with a new skill. The pathways available are well defined, and the prescribed Montessori methods by which they traverse are to be closely adhered to.

At any particular moment, each child is heading to a different place. Miss Carrie trusts that in using the Montessori approach as a map, the children will inch along their route to new learning, discovering new knowledge for themselves and course-correcting through the confusing twists and turns that punctuate the way. Miss Carrie is glad to periodically offer guidance to help them get turned back in the right direction when they find themselves off course. But at the end of the day, this trip is about the children—after all, this is the "Children's House." They are in the driver's seat and capable of getting themselves to their destinations.

4

MRS. TUCKER

Orchestrating Learning From "Oopses"

Anna Tucker's students are gathered on the floor in the meeting area of her kindergarten classroom. Each child is seated on one of several brightly colored squares within a neatly lined, rainbow-striped pattern on the rug. Mrs. Tucker sits in a pale turquoise chair situated to the right of a whiteboard easel on wheels, perched slightly above the heads of her students. She is a tall woman with fair skin and shoulder-length, straight brown hair that flips into a curl at the ends. Today, she is dressed in black from head to toe—black turtleneck sweater, black pants, and black dress boots. She rises and steps across the rug toward the window, grabbing a wooden stick with a black and gold pom-pom attached to the tip.

"We are going to play Catch My Oops," Mrs. Tucker says in a silly voice, her words lilting across the phrase. She shakes the pom-pom with each syllable as she marches back to her chair. As she settles back into her seat, she asks the students, "Are you ready?" The students' eyes are all turned toward her; she has their rapt attention. "I am going to write a sentence and there's going to be some oopses in there and you're going to have to catch them." She reaches toward the lower shelf of the whiteboard. "We have not gotten Bonkers out lately." Mrs. Tucker pulls out the old puppet, a wild creature with a red body, bright orange lips, yellow tufts of hair, and large bulging eyes, who—as she puts it—"looks like he's had a really rough day." She places it on her hand and launches into the game. "So, I'm going to write with the marker and then I'm going to

pass the marker to you. And you might get a chance to . . . Catch . . .
My . . . Oops! All right, let me put on my oops hat, which is pretty much
always on." She holds her head back for a moment and appears to be
thinking silently to herself as she continues to shake the pom-pom. "Let's
see. . . . Let me think, hmmm. . . . Ready." With those words, Mrs. Tucker
draws a vertical line on the board, then stops and says "too big," erasing
the line with a nearby towel.

One of the students calls out: "Oops!"

"Oops," echoes Mrs. Tucker. "I already oopsed." She reaches down to
the lower shelf of the whiteboard easel and draws out an oversized green
eraser from among the many items stored there. The word "OOPS!" is
printed on it in white, bolded, capital letters. "I better put this up because
I'm definitely going to be doing that." She places the eraser on the ledge
of the whiteboard easel and, with the students still quietly watching,
writes a simple sentence, which the class reads in chorus:

tobay Is Tuesday.

Hands go up around the room and someone calls out a guess. "If you see
an oops, raise your hand," says Mrs. Tucker. "Bonkers might let you
catch one of my oopses." She first calls Liam. "Find one of my oopses,"
she says, as he approaches the front of the room. Liam stands right up
near the board, about as close as he can get. She extends her hand toward
him and offers him a marker, telling him to "write on top of it to fix it."
Then, she whispers to Liam, "Trust yourself." With that small gesture of
encouragement, he adds a small loop on the left side of the lowercase *b* in
tobay, turning it into a lowercase *d*.

tocbay Is Tuesday.

"Nice!" affirms Mrs. Tucker. "Tell everyone. What was my oops?" Liam
steps to his right a little bit and points silently to the *b*. "It's not *tobay*,"
says Mrs. Tucker. "It should be—"

"—today," says Liam, finishing her sentence.

"Ding!" Her voice rings out, in celebration of Liam's correct answer.
"You caught one of my oopses." Liam returns to his seat and Mrs. Tucker
calls Stephania next. She jumps up from her seat on the floor and skips to

the front of the room, her thick, wavy, dark brown hair bouncing gently with each step. Once at the board, she draws a horizontal line over the top of the first letter of the sentence.

T̄oday Is Tuesday.

"What was wrong with my *t*, Stephania?" asks Mrs. Tucker.

"You did it well," she replies. "It was just a lowercase."

"Why does it matter, Stephania?" Mrs. Tucker inquires.

"Because it's supposed to be uppercase."

Bonkers starts to bounce as Mrs. Tucker talks. "Because it's the beginning—"

"—letter—" Stephania adds.

"—of a sentence," ends Mrs. Tucker. "That's right."

Next, Ryan is chosen to play. "What are you going to catch?" Mrs. Tucker asks.

Ryan walks up to the board, crosses out the *T* in Tuesday, and adds a small uppercase *M*.

T̄oday Is M✖uesday.

"Nice," says Mrs. Tucker. "What are you thinking? Tell everyone. What was my oops? Today is Tuesday." I have observed that Ryan is one of the shyest students in the class and speaks very softly; his voice is inaudible from where I am sitting across the classroom. Mrs. Tucker repeats what he has said. "So, you changed my *T* to an *M* because it's not Tuesday, it's . . ."

The children say in chorus: "Monday."

"Monday," she repeats. "Can I help you finish fixing that oops? Because I know it's a long word. Nice job, Ryan. Wow. . . . Ryan said that shouldn't be Tuesday, it should be Monday. He put the *M*. He's said, 'It's not Tuesday, Mrs. Tucker.'" She starts to write a word in red whiteboard marker, beginning with an uppercase *M*. "He says it should say . . ." She draws out the last word, prompting students to fill in the blank.

"Monday," says the class together, as she finishes writing the word just beneath the original sentence.

Todbay Is M✖uesday.

Monday

"Nicely done." Mrs. Tucker starts to look around at the class. "There is one more oops." Hands are up all across the room. "How about Mel," Mrs. Tucker whispers. Melissa stands up, quickly takes the marker from Mrs. Tucker, and stands silently in front of the board.

"Okay, send her brain mail. No voicemail, just brain mail." This is a phrase Mrs. Tucker spontaneously invented years ago in her classroom. She uses it as a way to protect think time, reminding the class not to call out with their voices, but instead to imagine they are sending their answers over to a fellow student, directly from one brain to another. There is not a sound in the room as students are sending brain mail to Melissa. She stands facing the whiteboard, her back to the class, marker in hand. Several seconds pass and she still does not write anything. Mrs. Tucker begins to chant, "Trust yourself, trust yourself," shaking the pom-pom with each word. The students quickly join in with her in support of their classmate. "If you're not sure," she says, "you may whisper to the front row." Melissa kneels down and consults with a couple of her classmates. Mrs. Tucker again starts chanting, "Trust yourself." Suddenly, Melissa jumps up and starts writing on the board.

"What's wrong with my beautiful *I*? I think you figured it out." Melissa writes a dot above the uppercase *I* in the word *Is* and Mrs. Tucker gasps.

Todbay İs M✖uesday.

Monday

"Mel! And why should it be lowercase?" She wrinkles her nose as she asks, "Is it the name of something?"

"No," replies Melissa. Mrs. Tucker wrinkles her nose again and quickly shakes her head left to right.

"Is it the beginning of the sentence?" Mrs. Tucker's nose remains wrinkled, head still shaking no.

"No . . . no," says Melissa, shaking her head left and right in sync with Mrs. Tucker. Melissa continues in a soft voice: "It's because it, it, it's the beginning of a sentence."

"Well this," says Mrs. Tucker, pointing to the *T* at the start of the word *Today*, "would be the beginning, right? This," she says, pointing to the letter *I*, "is in the middle of the sentence. So, I agree. . . . It should've looked like that." Mrs. Tucker writes the word *is*—all in lowercase—directly below the word in the original sentence. "And if it's easier to see this way—" It is silent as Mrs. Tucker takes a moment to write the word *Today* with an uppercase *T*, rendering the full sentence underneath the version just corrected by the students. "Help me read, please."

Todbay Is M✖️uesday.

Today is Monday

With Bonkers in hand, Mrs. Tucker points to the first word, cueing the class to join her. "Ready, set, . . ."

All together, they read the sentence as a class: "Today is Monday."

"And I just made another oops," she says, smiling. "Can anyone see my oops in the oops?"

After a couple of seconds of silence, Rachel suddenly sings out, "*Punctuation.*"

"Sing it again, Rachel," calls out Mrs. Tucker.

"*Punctuation!*" the class sings altogether, and Mrs. Tucker asks Felix to add a period, completing all of the corrections to the sentence.

Todbay Is M✖️uesday.

Today is Monday.

"Now you know how to play . . . Catch My Oops. Did you notice that one of your morning activities this week is a Catch My Oops every day? We will keep playing Catch My Oops. I'm going to leave the pom-pom here and Bonkers would like to say 'Bye! See you later!'"

Together, the children call out "Bye! See you later, Bonkers."

MEET THE MAESTRO: HOW MRS. TUCKER LEADS LEARNING FROM MISTAKES

From day one, Anna Tucker welcomes me into her kindergarten class-room with open arms. Each morning I am greeted with a warm smile and she seems very glad to see me, even commenting on several occasions how much she likes to have me there with her in the class. On my first morning in her classroom, she and the students sing their "Good Morning" song to me in chorus:

> *Good morning, good morning, good morning to you!*
> *Good morning, good morning, we're glad to see you!*

"*Good morning to you*," they all point at me at her prompting, and I smile.

"*Good morning to you!*" they continue, pointing in every which direc-tion at fellow students.

> *We sit in our places with sunshine-y faces,*
> *Oh, this is the way!*
> *To start a great day!*

I later find that there will be a personalized moment in the song to serenade me just about every time I am with the class for this morning meeting. And, in addition to being warmly greeted, I am routinely invited by Mrs. Tucker to grab food from her secret stash of snack bars, saltine crackers, and juice boxes; she welcomes me to place my belongings in her personal teacher closet behind her desk; and she asks me, along with the children, whether or not I'd like to place an order for a school lunch. Needless to say, I feel cared about and completely welcomed in the classroom community just about immediately due to Mrs. Tucker's warmth and kindness.

I quickly come to admire the way that Mrs. Tucker is not shy about facing mistakes as she skillfully instructs the twenty students in her kin-dergarten classroom. Drawing on her twenty-five years of teaching expe-rience—nineteen years in kindergarten and six years in a special educa-tion middle school—this veteran teacher frequently discusses, confronts, highlights, and even cheers the mistakes that she and her students make. "I think that the sign of a classroom that has a lot of learning going on, you're going to see a lot of mistakes. And they're not going to be quiet, and they're not going to be viewed as negative." She also feels kindergarten teachers hold one of the "most important" jobs in education. She believes that because "you're bringing them into a whole new environment . . . it's so key that you help them love coming to school and being excited and that they trust you and they like you." Helping them to be happy in school is her biggest goal, and she works to foster this in many ways, frequently turning to humor and games to infuse fun into the classroom.

Anna Tucker's kindergarten classroom is one of three at Houghton Elementary School, located in a suburb of the same metropolitan area as the other teachers. The school is located in one of the wealthiest towns in the area, which has an average household income approaching $100,000. The student body is more than 90 percent White, but the school does serve many international families. Although it is situated in a suburb, the school is easily accessible to the city—the on-ramp to a major highway sits just a two-minute drive away. Houghton is situated right in the center of a quiet, residential neighborhood, surrounded by moderately sized homes. The gray school building is spacious in its own right, flanked by sprawling playgrounds and fields used daily by the children during recess. Mrs. Tucker and the other kindergarten teachers have their own separate play area, fenced in and tucked to the side of the building, with easy access directly from their classrooms. Virtually every day that I visit, the class is given three outdoor recess sessions or "energy breaks" on this private playground. In addition, they also have at least thirty minutes of choice time daily, during which they can play anywhere in the classroom, pull out toys from home, and freely walk in and out of the cubby area where their private bathroom is located.

Over the weeks spent visiting her classroom, I observe that Mrs. Tucker's work with the students is like that of the conductor of a large orchestra. Each student plays their own individual instrument and the class functions as a mixed musical ensemble, exhibiting different strengths and weaknesses, levels of difficulty, and requirements for support in order to excel. The ensemble member who plays the oboe requires strong breath support and skill with circular breathing to create the proper tone with his reed. The way the standing bass player breathes is not important; instead, she must focus on supporting the physical weight of her instrument, plucking or bowing with adequate pressure, and carefully placing her fingers on the strings to produce a tone on pitch. And the ensemble member who plays the cymbals does not need to attend to breathing or finger placements, but instead must understand the mechanics of crashing metal, including how to start and stop its vibrations in a way that is harmonious with the dynamics of the musical piece and with her fellow players.

No one would expect the members of an orchestra to perfectly understand how instruments other than their own create their sound, but the maestro must understand the expression and technique of every instrument to collectively lead the group. In this way, Mrs. Tucker is the maestro of her class. Although the students receive the same prompt for most of their work, Mrs. Tucker attends closely to each individual learner's particular strengths and areas for improvement, holding them to their own individual standards and adapting instruction accordingly. As the students play their unique instruments of learning, Mrs. Tucker expects a few wrong notes or missed entrances, and wants them to be brave enough to just keep playing through the mistakes.

Mrs. Tucker describes this year's group of students as "the most challenging class I've ever had" in all her years of teaching. Throughout the day, she frequently shares comments with me privately about how loud or unsettled they are. Even the administration has acknowledged how difficult it is, allowing her aide, Mrs. Connor, to expand her hours from mornings to the full day on three days a week, and later increasing the time even more to include additional afternoons. Notably, in this particular year, an unusually high number of students in her class have individualized education plans (IEPs). These address a wide array of issues, including fine motor development, speech problems, anxiety, ADHD, social skills, and various academic needs. Some of the students with IEPs have charts in which they track how they are doing in each section of the day. Most receive pull-out interventions with specialists who come in and out of the classroom throughout the day and take students to another room for small group or individual teaching.

Behavior management is a big element in Mrs. Tucker's classroom, out of necessity. Over the years, she has learned effective ways to help students who have ADHD and emotional issues to improve their ability to focus in class. In addition to her direct correction—drawing to their attention that they are off task or doing something that bothers someone else—she always comes back to helping children help themselves get focused in order to learn. She frequently offers a host of options, available to everyone, to help students get recentered and plugged into the events of the moment. She has trifold cardboard displays that the children can use as an "office" to reduce their focus on visual distractions around them, defining their own space within the classroom. Any of the children are able to grab a special cushion to sit on, a "focus tool"—a small toy that often has a repetitive movement inherent to it—or an "idea clipboard" on which to write down words and images about moment-to-moment thoughts, rather than call out and interrupt a group discussion. Mrs. Tucker allows the students to monitor themselves and swap out or make adjustments as needed. She frequently will ask a question of a student who is calling out or squirmy, offering a chance for self-adjustment. "What do you need?" is a common inquiry, often followed by a few suggestions. "Do you need a focus tool?" "Do you have your idea clipboard?" At this point in the year, Will, Freddy, Felix, and Russ must have an idea clipboard for meetings at the circle, but others can also get them, if they choose. These four boys each have one stored in their chair pockets, and it is their personal responsibility to get these before each session.

Mrs. Tucker often uses metaphors and visualizations to convey what is expected of the children, particularly when it comes to feedback about behavior. To get them to stay quiet in large groups, she will remind them, "Lock your lips" or "Zip it, lock it, put it in your pocket." If something exciting happens, like winning a game they have played together, and she anticipates they'll want to cheer, she'll ask for a "silent squeal." And, if a student starts chatting or calling out during a group meeting, she might remind them to put "words into the finger" and down onto the paper on the idea clipboard to share with her later.

At times, a student may move around a lot with a case of "the wiggles," or feel "silly" and distracted, making it difficult to focus on the events in the classroom. In those instances, she may offer the child a short breather from the activity. This can take the form of "take 10"—a quick break during which they go into the coatroom and run around or take deep breaths as they count to ten—and then return to the group. Another method is telling them they can "catch a bus," where they go into the coatroom and run around in circles to get out their energy. Russ and Will often go for a walk around the hallway with Mrs. Connor or a class volunteer to step outside of the classroom into a different space where they can refocus.

Although it typically does not absorb a large portion of the whole-group learning time, Mrs. Tucker extends prompts multiple times a day to help trigger self-assessment and problem solving for the students to correct their own behavior using some of the available tools. This can be accomplished via a reminder of options, prompted through asking a question (e.g., "Do you need a focus tool?"). In other instances, she simply tells the students directly what to do (e.g., "Go take ten and come back ready to focus"), or she draws the child's attention to the behavior of peers for cues as to appropriate behavior (e.g., "They have an 'I'm trying to focus' face on"). The moments of correction are not always subtle but, as much as she can, Mrs. Tucker seems to try to put the agency in the student's hand. One day, when Rory is out of sorts as they are doing their writing practice, she says to her, "I'm going to ask you to stand up. Go look at yourself in the mirror in the bathroom, and see—do I have an 'I'm ready to work' face? Then come back; let me know." I watch Rory go off on her own and she returns about a minute and a half later, better able to continue her work.

Another demonstration of correction involves Drew, a student that Mrs. Tucker describes as "so lovable" but also "high maintenance." She feels that some teachers, past and future, might think it easy to simply say, "This kid is a problem," but Mrs. Tucker's intent is to "stop and take the time" to offer the support he needs. During one of the class meetings, I see that Drew has positioned himself with his back turned 180 degrees from the front of the classroom, the exact opposite direction of his classmates. In response, Mrs. Tucker softly calls to him: "Drew, can you find my eyes? Would you like a cushion from under my desk?" He turns his head toward her momentarily, and then his eyes again begin to drift away from her. "Hey blue eyes! Blue eyes!" she calls out to him. His head pivots back, and he again makes eye contact with her. She smiles and asks, "Would you like a cushion?" He starts to silently shake his head left to right, indicating no, then quickly changes to bob his head up and down, indicating yes. "It's up to you," she says. "There's a couple different kinds under my desk. Help yourself." Mrs. Tucker then resumes the class activity, and Drew is free to meander over to her desk in his own time, select the cushion of his liking, and bring it back over to rejoin the group with increased focus. Drew independently gets what he needs for himself, as Mrs. Tucker continues on with what she was saying.

Offers like this are extended frequently in Mrs. Tucker's classroom. She says that she does not always want to be "giving . . . negative directions about what to do." Instead, she focuses on helping the students to better understand and track themselves. "We all need to learn to take ten . . . they figure out that isn't a punishment so much as 'my body needs something right now, or my brain.'" Rather than create a big, negative moment, she allows students "to remove themselves for a minute [and] get it together," while at the same time "trying to keep it seamless" with respect to the progress in the class activity or discussion. It is as if Mrs. Tucker—the conductor at the podium in front of the orchestra—makes a subtle request of the bass drum player, but allows him to resolve it himself, without specific directives on technique. She trusts that the student, with the prior experience from earlier practice, knows how to adjust for himself.

Across the average day that I am in the room, the class transitions smoothly from whole-group activities or discussions into individual seatwork. The routine and structure of the class is generally very prescribed. There are a finite number of activities that the children will do in her class and set ways of doing them that they all know by now, within the second half of the academic year. During the work time, Mrs. Tucker gives them a "score" that maps out just what they need to do or practice. The students are often given materials to be used in specific ways: a craft for which they have to cut out a pig-shaped sheet, later threading through a thin strip of paper that slides to make various pig family words; a packet of blank pages with open space and several lines that they can use for a week or two to write sentences and draw illustrations during writing exercises; or an often-referenced card in their chair pockets that lists several common sight words.

Mrs. Tucker's classroom has a great deal of infrastructure that affords her substantial time each day to check in with students individually and in small groups. She has an expectation that all of the parents will sign up to volunteer regularly in the classroom. This means that, within that rotation, one of the students in her class has a mom or dad (and sometimes a younger sibling, too) in the room every morning of the week during the dedicated forty-five minute shared reading and independent writing time. She also has a general school volunteer, who rotates around to different classrooms and comes into her class during the same forty-five-minute block. Daily, Mrs. Tucker's team includes a parent volunteer, the school volunteer, and Mrs. Connor—the class aide. This means that there are commonly four adults circulating as the students do seatwork each morning, usually focused on writing and/or reading activities. Simply having more people present in the room certainly does not guarantee excellent teaching; however, when paired with Mrs. Tucker's experience and skill in teaching and good management of the extra hands on deck, there are huge benefits to the children's learning experience—namely, more individualized attention. Most often, the volunteers move around to check with the children as Mrs. Tucker flits about the room, moving briskly from one student to the next, sharing a quick bit of feedback, tossing out ideas about how to correct mistakes, or suggesting a next step that will help improve a skill.

I am impressed with the way that Mrs. Tucker's pleasant demeanor is somehow simultaneously serene and enthusiastic, no matter what the children do or say. Typically, her facial expression is relaxed and neutral with an occasional smile, and her eyes exude calmness. She never yells; her voice is consistently somewhere in the range of a moderate level down to a soft whisper. Somehow, she also remains animated and engaged, conveying with her words that she is paying close attention to what the students are doing and saying. I imagine this requires a great deal of self-awareness and ability to genuinely appear cool, calm, and collected, despite the frenzy within the energetic classroom.

FLEXIBLY INTERPRETING THE SCORE

Day after day, as I sit in Mrs. Tucker's class, I notice that although she is not timid about telling the students about mistakes, she rarely tells them directly they are wrong or provides them with the right answer. Instead, she demonstrates an adaptive approach to corrections. "We just try to keep everything light. The stakes are not high here." Student mistakes prompt questions and curiosity, and she is often generous with the time she allows children to puzzle through to a guess.

Furthermore, Mrs. Tucker shares with me that, in many cases, she does not view the mistakes students make as something wrong. This sentiment ties to her focus on flexibility—a concept she references multiple times a day. Although the bulk of tasks she offers are well-defined, the class is flexible with their schedule, frequently shifting and reordering to skip things they don't have time to do, and adding more time to finish other things, as needed. Similarly, she is flexible with answers, feeling that most of her questions allow a wide spectrum of acceptable responses. "I guess in kindergarten, I don't really think of there being a lot of errors, because I try to make kindergarten a gray area. There's so many ways you can come at this. And there's really more outcomes than even adults think there can be."

When students make mistakes with academic concepts—writing a letter backward, adding two numbers together incorrectly, guessing the wrong letter sound—Mrs. Tucker tends to respond by drawing out the interaction. She will slow them down, sometimes singing *"hold your horses"* to prompt them to start over and take their time this go-around. At other times, she will affirm the challenge: "Watch out, those rascals are trying to trick you" or "Yeah, that's such a hard word, isn't it?" When it involves mistakes related to a student's academic learning and skill building, she makes it a point to never "sugarcoat things or ignore them or pretend they didn't happen"—she faces them head on, in partnership with the student, supporting the child's own inquiry about how to figure out what went wrong.

Although many answers are more black and white—3 + 4 always equals 7—Mrs. Tucker uses questions to probe student reasoning and to process how they came to a particular answer. She protects their think time as they ponder their mistakes and is generous in giving them credit for reasonable thinking and logic. She also wants "the kids to feel like they can ask anything." Mrs. Tucker models this with most interactions in the classroom, demonstrating how their learning process is interactive. Even after they land on an answer, that doesn't mean they have to stop there.

Mrs. Tucker draws attention to their mistakes, as well as her own, and she models how to take it in a positive way. She says, "I try to go out of my way to make sure the kids are feeling like, 'It's okay to make oopses.' And here, I make them, too." Many times, she will tell a child who is having a hard time dealing with the fact he or she messed up to "be flexible with yourself." She feels that being transparent about mistakes is important to do in kindergarten because, in her opinion, "If you can't be taught this is a good time to make mistakes, when is it ever going to happen, you know? It's not like all of a sudden in third grade, 'Okay, you can oops now' but for four years you thought you couldn't. . . . I feel like now is the time." She invests heavily in growing children's comfort with mistakes, building a positive classroom culture with a foundation of humor, flexibility, and emotional safety, while making substantial investments in classroom camaraderie.

While she certainly wants students to feel comfortable making mistakes, Mrs. Tucker enacts some clear instructional moves related to whether and how long she and/or the class will address a given mistake. The pace of these interactions varies depending on the type of mistake. When individual students are making behavioral or social mistakes related to classroom management—for example, calling out without raising their hands; singing or talking loudly in a disruptive manner—Mrs. Tucker tends to keep the pace of the exchange brisk, the words spoken softly or even exchanged nonverbally, through gestures or writing.

However, in almost every other situation, Mrs. Tucker tends to draw out her response to mistakes, lengthening it with extended dialogue in which the students are actively involved. This is true in the case of individual academic correction, as well as whole-class social/behavioral redirection. If the energy of the entire class is high, she keeps a pulse on that and may even redirect the entire plan for instruction. For example, one day when the class is preparing to transition to a new activity, Mrs. Tucker looks around. I notice that several of the children are talking to each other, with their attention turned away from her. She checks in with them, reminding everyone that "if you're in this class, it's your responsibility, your job, to learn and let others learn. If you are not ready to learn or let others learn, I do not want you sitting with us right now." She then prompts the students to do some internal self-reflection: "Ask yourself, 'Am I ready to learn?'" and "Ask yourself, 'Am I ready to let others learn?'" After giving the class a couple of moments to think about each question, she asks them, "Was there anyone who told themselves, 'No, I'm not ready to learn?'" Immediately, Freddy's hand shoots up. "You're not? Okay, what do you need so you can get ready?" Freddy chooses to go to the calm corner. As he steps away from the meeting, Mrs. Tucker asks, "Is there anyone else who told themselves, 'No, I'm not ready?'" One by one, many other hands go up.

"Can I look at a book?"

"I want to go to the cubby."

"I feel a little silly."

"I feel a little silly, too."

Mrs. Tucker pauses. "I'm noticing a lot of silly. Do we need to do some kind of silly song?"

"Yeah," the class cries out in chorus.

Mrs. Tucker holds up the book. "The book is going to wait." She gets the attention of the student helper and asks, "Would you like *Beanbag Rock* or *Count Off*?" The class momentarily abandons the original plan— reading centers—and instead takes a break to dance to the *Count Off* music track.

This moment—and many others on an almost daily basis—demonstrates how Mrs. Tucker sets a measured pace in the class, while remaining adaptive and flexible. She shapes the day's routine based on what the students need and what, in her assessment, they are capable of doing in their present state of mind. "I really think that if kids are really tired or really excited for something, you need to go in that direction." In this case, the students are not offering attention and are talking over her. Rather than interpret their behavior as individual mistakes to be corrected, she reads it as information about the internal state of the students and, in turn, she responds with what she feels they need—a prompt to self-assess how they are doing internally and an invitation to take a break, if they need it. As I observe this moment in the class, I can see that it is necessary, but also ponder the extent to which this is a luxury. Although any teacher can take a break, Mrs. Tucker arguably takes the types of breaks that are only options because she is afforded close physical access to the playground and autonomy to adjust her schedule as she sees fit. It is the students who benefit from this level of adaptability. Leaning on the structures provided by their teacher, they have opportunities to take risks and play with new ideas as they are learning, and to change the pace as needed.

SUPPORTING INDIVIDUAL PLAYERS TO BUILD THE ENSEMBLE

According to Mrs. Tucker's assessment of the students in her classroom, she has "twenty sets of goals going on. I do not have one set of goals that I apply to all these kids." And, she adds, "I just shouldn't be a teacher, if I do." The identification of and support for individual standards and goals are central to her work. Because much of the seatwork in the class is done independently, she is able to circulate and quietly give feedback in a one-on-one interaction, allowing her to "keep everything on their level" as she moves from child to child to offer comments and suggestions for improvement. This is important because as she works with "the more mature or the academically more capable kids," she wants "them to feel like there's areas that they need to work on," but doesn't "want the kid over here next door who's struggling with two words to even be thinking about some of this stuff." With this approach, ideally everyone can get the feedback they need, at the level they need it.

Benjamin Zander, the conductor of the Boston Philharmonic Orchestra, once said, "The conductor of an orchestra doesn't make a sound. He depends on his ability to make other people powerful." Mrs. Tucker—as the conductor of her class's learning—empowers her pupils to exercise their current academic capabilities. She invests time in helping the children adjust their expectations for themselves so that they can thrive in their individual learning. This can mean shifting the goal of an activity down to an easier level or pushing themselves to do something more challenging; and it varies widely from one child to another. It is important to Mrs. Tucker that the children have a sense of what they can do, and what is appropriate for them to expect of themselves. "I want them all to not care what anyone else sitting next to them is doing and just feel like they can make those mistakes." Part of that is helping them to adjust their expectations for what they can do now and looking ahead to goals in the future without worry of what they cannot do now.

This manifests in her work with them during their literacy activities. After listening to Mrs. Tucker read through a chapter or two of a book, she tells the students to independently write sentences reflecting facts or scenes from the story. In this context, she makes several distinctions about what she expects from them. For example, she makes it clear that she does not expect them to spell things the same way that she does:

> I make a big deal about kindergarten spelling versus grown-up spelling. And before they do something like the writing prompt . . . I'll say, "Who's going to write like a kindergartener?" And they raise their hands, and then I'll say, "Who's going to write like an adult?" My aide and I will raise our hands. . . . And I'll say, "You know what? I've been doing this forty years longer than you have," and they're like, "Wow."

In this sense, she directly gives them permission to spell using just the skills they have and not to worry about what it's "supposed" to look like. She just expects them to "do the kindergarten spelling and I'm going to do the grown up." By framing herself as someone who has decades of experience, Mrs. Tucker is reminding them—before they even make mistakes or try out the skills they have—that they have permission to be at their current ability level; and they should not expect the same results as the teacher.

While Mrs. Tucker, in some cases, helps students to strive for more reasonable standards, she sometimes urges them to go for a more difficult challenge. A common phrase she says to students when she checks their work is "You're getting smarter and I'm getting harder." It is reserved for moments in which a child executes a task at a level below their potential. This is an extension of her focus on individual standards because, with this feedback, she directs students to choose harder challenges for themselves next time. When they are writing sentences on their own during writing practice, Felix's goal is to try to write the first letter sound of each word, and to correctly represent the number of words by drawing a horizontal line for each word. He is praised for his efforts on this and she encourages him for his progress. However, when she checks Russ's paper, she asks him to do an additional sentence. Looking at his paper, she comments, "That is really working for you. Well, since you're getting smarter, I'm getting . . ."

"Harder," Russ replies.

"Great!" says Mrs. Tucker. "One more sentence, Mr. Smarty Brain."

At other times, she draws on her knowledge of the student's prior performance to help them reassess their own capabilities. On a day when Rory writes a single sentence, Mrs. Tucker asks her to skim the prior pages of her writing notebook and take a closer look. "Look at all the sentences. Look at all this, look at all this." Mrs. Tucker flips through her notebook. "That's why I'm confused by this." She flips to the current page for today's work, revealing the one sentence Rory has written thus far. "This is a great start, but you just did a teeny tiny one today. I know how smart you are. So, you're getting smarter, I'm getting . . . harder."

In this class, the reward for progress and strong performance is praise and increased challenge. In these interactions, particularly with Russ and Rory, their final product does not match prior levels of performance, nor do they make any mistakes. "Kids are so competitive, so I'm going to feed into that in a positive way, like 'You know what? I know how smart you are.'" While other students in the class are done with one sentence, and although Rory is encouraged in the good start to how she begins her work, she gets a clear message that the task is not complete for her because her potential is greater than what she displays on that given day.

Moments like these demonstrate that Mrs. Tucker is truly interested in promoting the children's ability to do for themselves. Making the "obvious mistakes" is a means to help them learn. "To me, those are expected, natural. . . . That's the good mistakes to be making." As they make the good mistakes, she gives the feedback needed for them to know they made a mistake, but the space and freedom to counter back and share what they think is right. Sometimes, the answer is black and white—what is the next letter of the alphabet? What does a given letter sound like? If the student got it wrong, there is no way around it. But she tries to follow the student's logic to see how they landed on a particular answer.

One day, Mrs. Tucker introduces the Alphabet Sock Game (an activity that Mrs. Tucker had recently invented) to help practice letter recognition. The children form a large rectangle around the room of the meeting area, as the floor is covered with many brightly colored footprints. Each paper has an uppercase and lowercase letter printed on it. Mrs. Tucker selects a couple of student volunteers to help her play the game. Rory and Edward are chosen—one girl and one boy. They start by looking for the letter *A*, and Mrs. Tucker and the two students shuffle over to that letter. Then, the next letter is called, and they shuffle over to that letter. In this game, there are a couple of times when Mrs. Tucker explicitly counters the student's guess. They make their way through the alphabet beginning at *A* and eventually end up at *Q*.

"See if you can find it," says Mrs. Tucker. She and the students are turning around, scanning the floor for the next letter that comes after *Q*. Edward, one of her helpers, is searching fervently. "Hold on, let him think, let him think."

After searching for a few moments, Edward looks up at Mrs. Tucker and asks, "*U*?" while standing on the foot-shaped foam piece.

"I disagree!" shouts Mrs. Tucker, sounding excited and happy. "This is a fantastic, wait, wait . . . *Q*."

"That's a *U*!" someone exclaims energetically from the border of the rug.

"But I think that's why he thought so," Mrs. Tucker explains. "Because *Q* and *U* are always together. Someone, we're stuck on *U*. Look at the alphabet?" She points up at the alphabet chart, and the class starts singing the ABC song at turbo speed, a strategy she has modeled to troubleshoot mix-ups made earlier in the game.

"*A, B, C, D, E, F, G . . .*" Eventually they make their way back to the end of the alphabet. "*. . . L, M, N, O, P, Q, R . . .*"

"*R*?" Mrs. Tucker asks, verifying the next letter.

"It's right there, it's right there, it's right there!" calls out Justin, jumping to his feet and pointing at the letter card. The class continues the game, making their way through to the end of the alphabet to the letter *Z*.

While there are times in which Mrs. Tucker provides the needed correction (e.g., *U* does not come immediately after *Q*), there are other times when Mrs. Tucker is adamant about convincing students to change their responses for themselves. This may happen through prolonged discussion and prompts to self-evaluate and is particularly important at times when the answers are more objective. For example, the reading and writing curriculum Mrs. Tucker is required to use "want[s] kids to track" the work they are doing in the classroom and to "have a personal goal." She decides that the task is a bit too complex and time consuming and, because it "is just not going to happen" as prescribed, she decides to "tweak it" so that it will work better for her students. Every two weeks, "I come up with four work goals, four social goals," and in small groups, she allows each child to consider and choose what they want to try to improve. The work goals can include different kindergarten academic skills (e.g., use of capitalization and punctuation), and social goals often have to do with self-regulation and interacting with others (e.g., managing volume of own voice in the classroom).

One morning I hear Mrs. Tucker share with the class that "everyone is going to sign up for a work goal and a social goal." During a relaxation time, she calls over small groups of three or four children to talk about which goals are the best fit, helping them narrow things down to a smaller number of choices. Once they identify a goal that they want to take on, each child signs underneath the goal on a sheet to be publicly posted in their classroom.

Near the end of the time, after toggling between work and social goals and cycling through several small groups, it is finally Ashley's turn. She is a small, quiet girl with long dark hair pulled back into a ponytail. She sits across from Mrs. Tucker as they weigh the options for which individual goal Ashley should pursue.

"Calm and quiet in the coatroom. I didn't know you were ever loud and crazy," Mrs. Tucker says.

Ashley looks at her with a smile. Mrs. Tucker slides the paper back over toward Ashley again. "It's up to you," she says. "You know more than me what you need help with." They review the options again, and Mrs. Tucker elaborates on why other goals might be a better fit.

"What about speaking up and sharing your great ideas? You've been doing that a lot lately," she comments, implying that Ashley might already have a handle on that social skill. "You tell me." Ashley turns her head left and right, looking across the four options placed in front of her. After a few seconds of silent thinking, Mrs. Tucker chimes back in. "Do you think it's speaking up? Not interrupting?" Mrs. Tucker wrinkles her nose and shakes her head no. "Do you agree—that's okay already, right?" Ashley shakes her head up and down in a very gentle nod. "Do you feel like in the coatroom you get a little loud and crazy?" Mrs. Tucker looks at Ashley. She is quiet for a moment, then shakes her head left to right a few times, so gently that although I am sitting just a few feet away, I can just barely discern it as shaking her head no.

"Not so much." Mrs. Tucker moves on. "Okay. Telling kids when you don't like something or speaking up? Which one did you want to work on this week?"

Ashley silently points to the page with the goal of speaking up, as she looks up at her teacher. Mrs. Tucker gives a nod and, with a quick move, plops a pencil on the table right in front of Ashley. "You have really started doing that lately. That's a good choice." Ashley remains silent as she leans forward to write her name on the page and then leaves the table.

Mrs. Tucker really likes the goals because the children get a chance to choose from "what they think is appropriate" and, fortunately, she finds that "they almost always pick what is at their level." This is the case for Ashley, who meekly selects the goal of speaking up, although she is a shy child. Mrs. Tucker walks her through a process of considering each option, but at the end of the day, Ashley chooses for herself and signs her name below the goal. The list is later posted in the classroom for reference in the coming days. This is an example of Mrs. Tucker's attempts to help students take on making decisions for themselves. "Even if I was sort of hoping they'd pick this one and they really want this one, if they can tell me why, then they're taking ownership, and it doesn't matter what goal *I* want that week." In life, the students won't always have a maestro like Mrs. Tucker conducting them as they navigate through their learning.

CENTER STAGE: EXPECTING AND INSPECTING SOLO PERFORMANCES OF MISTAKES

Part of helping students own their learning is to work individually with them, to let them try to figure out what happened, and then allow them to self-correct. Frequently, this process happens as Mrs. Tucker is sitting with a child at a table, exchanging hushed phrases while huddled over a worksheet, pencils in hand. But it is relatively common for her to make these one-on-one interactions public, transforming an individual student's moment of misunderstanding into a featured exposition for the whole class. This reminds me of the way that the conductor, during an orchestra performance, selects one individual to play a solo for a section of the composition, as the rest of the orchestra continues along in the background. For the player, it can be both anxiety-provoking and thrilling to be featured in front of the crowd. On more than one occasion in Mrs. Tucker's classroom, I watch her feature several children's mistakes prominently before the audience of the full class. Mrs. Tucker conjures that same sense of amazement as I watch her call attention to student mistakes, drawing all of the children's eyes from around the room squarely onto their peer's "fantastic oops." She always frames it as an opportunity and an honor for them to be a "soloist," guiding them along as they play out their mistakes for a minute or two in front of the class.

I observe one such solo performance on a morning when Mrs. Tucker is updating the schedule to reflect the day's upcoming activities. She asks for a little help from Lionel, who has been working on his letter-sound matches. Mrs. Tucker gives him a chance to practice these skills by asking him to replace the card representing the day of the week.

"Lionel, tell yourself 'I need Monday' . . . *muh*." Mrs. Tucker hands Lionel a stack of white cards. "*Muh* . . . Monday."

As Lionel sifts through the cards, Mrs. Tucker chats with the class about the specials for the day. Then, suddenly, Lionel holds up a card toward Mrs. Tucker. His selection has the word *Wednesday* printed on it in black, hand-printed letters. "Ooooo. Nice try!" she says, pointing at him with an eyebrow raised and a slight smile on her face. "That would be an upside-down *m*." Lionel shifts the cards around quickly, placing the Monday card on top, then offers up the stack toward Mrs. Tucker.

"Yes, yes," she says to him. "Trust yourself. Fantastic." She reaches out and takes the cards from Lionel's small hands. Then, she addresses the full class. "Can I show you this really great oops Lionel just had? Totally understand this oops," she adds, sympathetically shaking her head and looking over at him. "Check it out. Really great oops." She holds the Wednesday card in her right hand and the Monday card in her left hand, with both cards facing the students. Before them, they see the words *Monday* and *Wednesday*. "Think silently in your head for a second. Why was this a great oops?"

The room pauses for a few seconds of silence, then a student calls out, "'Cause, 'cause he saw it upside down."

Mrs. Tucker makes a surprised gasp. "Wait a second!" she replies. "That looks a lot like an *M* and especially if you go like—" She turns the Monday card upside down and places it right next to the *W* on the Wednesday card. From my view, the letter shapes look just the same. "So, Lionel—fantastic oops. Nice job."

In this moment, Mrs. Tucker gives Lionel a chance to try out something in front of the class. When he makes a "fantastic oops," she first lets him know that he made a mistake and gives him the space to correct it. Then, after the entire process of trying, making a mistake, and self-correcting has taken place, Mrs. Tucker does a slo-mo replay of what happened in front of everyone. This includes first allowing him the chance to self-correct once he is aware of his mistake. Then, she talks about it at length, giving a sense of why this is a reasonable mistake—that is, *M* and *W* do make the same shape; they are mirror images of each other and therefore easier to mix up. Through this play-by-play recap, she offers an opportunity for Lionel to think through his thought process, and to serve as a reminder for other students who might be likely to make similar mistakes in the future.

Another example of how Mrs. Tucker has the class correct mistakes comes up during their daily letter-writing practice. In these sessions, the children are focusing most of their energy on their own whiteboards, drawing lines and loops to practice their letters. Mrs. Tucker is a real stickler about how they draw the letters—which lines come first, in which direction do they go. She says that she does this because "the reality is . . . these kids have to be up and running and trying to do letters so quickly" and "this is the age where their pencil grip is going to start." As a result of these beliefs, she works hard to get them to be precise in the sequence of strokes, and they practice it every day. Sometimes she tells them things like "I don't mean to be picky, but I need to know that you know how to do it." She feels that, given the expectations in first grade and beyond, this focus on writing is important. Otherwise, "if I let them make those habits now, it's going to be really hard to break later."

On one particular day, after observing the students working, I watch Mrs. Tucker give a refresher on how to draw capital letters *L* and *E*. Mrs. Tucker is standing in front of the class, next to the whiteboard easel with a red marker in hand. "Okay, tell me what to do."

"Top start, pull down." As the students call out the directions, she touches the tip of the marker to the easel and slides it down, making a single vertical line on the board.

"Down," she echoes. "Do you want me to lift yet? Pull down, slide across, now lift." She has made an uppercase *L* and turns to face the class. "Now where?" she asks.

L

Someone calls out, "Up top."

"Top start, slide across." She draws the top line of the letter *E*. It looks like a tall rectangle with the right side missing.

⌐

From the group, another student calls out the next step. "Middle start."

"Middle start?" Her eyes widen slightly. "Okay," she agrees, "I'll do a middle start." Mrs. Tucker follows the directive exactly. Without lifting, she slides her marker from the top right, down toward the middle left, leaving a diagonal trail between.

The students laugh out loud. "Noooooo!"

"*You forgot to tell me to lift,*" sings Mrs. Tucker, making a funny face as she erases the letter with the oops. "*Try again,*" she sings. "Action! Top start, pull down." She starts to draw as she recaps the directions.

"Lift!" someone calls out.

"Slide across," she continues. She makes the top line again. "*Now* lift. Now what?" Her hand is suspended a couple of inches away from the board, her eyes are looking out at the class.

Several reply, "Top start."

In response, she touches her pen to the whiteboard. "Justin, help me. . . . Slide across. Thank you." She draws the top line and pauses with her marker on the board.

"Lift," say the students in chorus.

"Lift," repeats a smiling Mrs. Tucker, eyes wide as she says the word. "Middle start, slide across." She draws in the final line, leaving an upper-case *E* behind on the whiteboard. "Start like an *L*, and then you can totally do an *E*." She snaps the marker closed and calls out "Action!" signaling that it is the children's turn to try out the method on their own.

In this instance, Mrs. Tucker is doing this group practice intervention in response to individual mistakes she has seen while circulating in the room. She extends continuous opportunities for students to guide the process. When the students make mistakes, she does not correct them, but instead renders them in plain sight, providing a chance for them to identify the error and collectively correct it.

Mrs. Tucker frequently reminds students that learning can be difficult and that mistakes are expected. These messages are often shared in passing as children are working and infused into the feedback she shares with them as they work. Her efforts remind me of a conductor who has previewed a musical score and gives the orchestra advance notice about a difficult part ahead; I often see Mrs. Tucker give her students a heads-up about the impending challenges inherent to the tasks they are taking on. On several occasions during the time I am in her class, she refers to the trickiness of a task when a student makes a mistake—placing the blame on the task itself rather than on the student's ability or effort. When children make reversals while printing their letters, she is quick to praise them for the correct parts of their work, and then playfully adds—as an aside—feedback that the figure was reversed: "Turn around, you rascal *j*." This directive for the student to tell the letter to "turn around" comes up often when kids write reversals for letters and numbers, like *j*, *D*, *3*, and *7*. When Kelsey corrects her own number sentence, Mrs. Tucker comments, "It is so easy for those rascal threes to look the other way. You have to say, 'Turn around, you threes!'" Or, there is another time when Rory writes out an addition sentence during morning meeting. Mrs. Tucker tells her, "Two numbers are trying to trick you. Don't let them do it." Once Rory identifies the mistake—two reversed numeral fours—Mrs. Tucker says to her and the class, "It is so easy for those numbers to turn around." Personifying the mistake brings levity to the feedback. Watching these interactions, it seems to me that it is not about something that Kelsey or Rory did wrong; it is about reminding them to be on the lookout for the tricks that numbers and letters play on you when you are writing.

When students sound out words during reading or writing, Mrs. Tucker often draws to their attention how the English language is confusing, and she highlights how the spellings are not intuitive. For instance, one day while collecting lunch orders from the class, Mrs. Tucker asks the class, "How do you spell pizza?" In that interaction, she acknowledges that it looks like "*pih-zuh*," "it sounds like *p-eeT-zuh*," and "if I was writing it, . . . I might've said . . . *peeeet-suh*." In the end, she closes the discussion of the word *pizza* by telling the students that it is spelled like "*pih-za* 'cause, I told you, English doesn't make sense."

Another time, when the class is coming up with words in the *-ot* word family (e.g., rot, hot, cot), Will suggests the letter *y*. Immediately, Mrs. Tucker says in front of the whole class, "This is a great, this is a fantastic oops, and he is not even going to even understand why it's an oops because English is confusing." She makes a big deal of it, first confirming with Will, "By *yot* you mean a boat, right?" and then asking, "Do you want to know what *yot* looks like?" The children seem curious and, again, she explains how this doesn't make sense.

"Crazy, I don't know who invented the English language. "*Yot*," she says, picking up a marker and starting to write on a sheet of paper. "You're going to say 'Mrs. Tucker, that has to be wrong.' It should be wrong. But this," she declares, turning her paper around and revealing the spelling of the word, "is what *yacht* looks like in English."

"What?" calls out one student softly. Will is smiling, and the rest of the children remain quiet and focused on her as she continues her explanation.

"It looks like *yaa-chuh-tuh*. But for some reason they say *yot*." Mrs. Tucker raises her hands and shrugs her shoulders, saying, "I don't know why but for some reason, Joe Schmoe was having a bad day when he invented that word."

In both the *pizza* and *yacht* examples, Mrs. Tucker thoroughly justifies the children's mispronunciation, misspelling, and general confusion about the letter-sound matching as something outside of their control. They are at the mercy of decisions made by a generic "Joe Schmoe," who came up with all of these strange spellings. By talking about what a word would sound like based on what they know of the letters and their accompanying sounds, Mrs. Tucker also makes a case to the class for why they need to learn certain snap words—also known as sight words or "watch-out words"—in her classroom. At one point, she explains that they are called snap words "because you should know them in a snap," and they can't be sounded out correctly applying their knowledge of letter sounds. For example, the letter *s* "is wearing a *Z* costume" in the word *was*; otherwise, it would be pronounced "*wass*." And if they sounded out the word *you*, it would sound like "*yaah-uh*." Although this conveys an expectation of having them memorized, she clarifies that this "doesn't mean you should come to kindergarten and already know them. It means once I teach them to you, . . . I don't want you to sound them out." Actually, she says, "they don't make sense if you sound them out" because "someone decided let's confuse kindergarteners and make these words look really weird." As with the rascally letters and numbers, the blame for children's mistakes with snap words is shifted to a distant writer of the English language, who was purposely trying to mix them up. This helps soften the blow of making mistakes and makes the errors less personal and more pedestrian.

It is worth noting that Mrs. Tucker offers a lot of affirming words with the students, regardless of whether they get something right on the first try. She also takes care to point out the details of the feedback after praise. When a mistake is made, she will lead with words like "Gorgeous," "Terrific," "Nicely done," "I'm impressed," and then follow up with "One thing I'll say is . . ." or "Only thing is . . ." Further, Mrs. Tucker frequently expresses that she is impressed with them and that they are smart, as evidenced by their attention on different tasks in their work. In one of our interviews, she explains, "I never say, 'Right' . . . 'wrong.' . . . It's 'Wow!' 'Really good guess' or 'Almost.' . . . I just want them to really feel like they can take the chances and just start to trust themselves." Commonly in these instances, the praise is framed in a way that propels the child into the next try.

- "Whoa. Impressive, Mr. Townsend. Wow! Okay, go again!"
- "Don't forget to impress me with punctuation."
- "Great, one more sentence, Mr. Smarty Brain."
- "Pat yourself on the back. I just caught you reading. I don't want to hear any of this bologna about I can't read. You just did it."

There is a call to action in these celebratory moments. It is not simply about Mrs. Tucker letting them know whether they got something correct in the moment but laying the groundwork for the next task. In this way, she leverages those successes as fuel to motivate her students to take a shot again the next time, to try to rise to tackle the next challenge, or to show what they can do on another skill. Even if there is not a response needed at that exact moment, praising the effort is an investment toward the next time that student is standing up there, nervous about sharing. It can be a reference point to encourage them to take a stab at it next time.

Also, even when they have made a mistake, she tends to acknowledge the parts of what the children said that are right. In that sense, they get partial credit for what they *can* do. For example, during an activity in which the children are practicing word families, Mrs. Tucker lets Kelsey get involved in pronouncing some of the roots. She is sitting in her rocking chair at the front of the class and holds up a star-shaped, blue foam flashcard, showing her the letter *o* and letter *p* that represent the *-op* family. "Uh—Kelsey, let's go to you, sweetie," she says. "How do you say that?" Mrs. Tucker slowly holds up the card while looking at Kelsey.

"*Ohp*," says Kelsey, pronouncing it as in the word *hope*.

"Good guess," affirms Mrs. Tucker. "If there was a silent *e*, you'd be absolutely right."

"*Op*," calls out Freddy, this time pronounced as in the word *stop*.

Mrs. Tucker stretches the stack of stars in her hand toward Freddy. "Good job. The *op* family."

In this example, Kelsey is given the opportunity to try, is offered clear feedback so that she knows she didn't get this one correct, but she also receives affirmation that she does know something relevant. The pace of the interaction is swift—and Mrs. Tucker continues giving other children chances to try. It is a moment that is positive, but the class does not dwell on Kelsey's particular oops. This moment really illustrates another aspect of Mrs. Tucker's perspective on mistakes—responses can differ along with circumstances. Sometimes, as in the case of Kelsey's mispronunciation, Mrs. Tucker is swift in moving past them, keeping the discussion "in the moment, and 'Let's move on.' Don't focus on them too much." But at other times when someone makes a "fantastic oops," she chooses to feature mistakes, asking the whole class to look at them. I find it interesting to consider the expertise needed to know, on the fly, when each approach is warranted. These moments are almost always impromptu. And, when they do happen, she has to first identify the mistake as one worth dwelling on, then assess the child's level of openness to being showcased and, finally, determine the best way to guide the interaction. This feat truly requires skill.

LISTENING CAREFULLY FOR OFF-KEY NOTES: TEACHER AND STUDENT CHECKS FOR MISTAKES

I notice that Mrs. Tucker spends a great deal of time scanning student worksheets or whiteboards. She has shared with me that she is looking at both their process and their work activities, to assure that they are edging toward the understanding she wants them to have. In addition to checking the level at which they can perform, she also cares about the process of how they think and do their work. This includes her belief that the way she interacts with a child about a mistake will influence the overall class dynamics. "If someone's having trouble in the room, how you respond to them, they're all hyper aware of that . . . I do have to be very careful how I respond, then, 'cause that's how the kids are going to figure that. . . . You're creating the culture of the classroom."

Mrs. Tucker sets the tone in her classroom, taking several specific approaches to shape that classroom culture as it relates to mistakes, including frequent, close monitoring with feedback, creating opportunities for students to try again after practice, and infusing humor into the interaction. This is well demonstrated in the sessions the class has each day to practice their letters. Just before lunch, each of the children pick up a whiteboard, a marker, and an eraser, and go to work writing the focal letters for the day. Typically, they start their work with the aide, and are usually well into it when Mrs. Tucker enters the room. The students are spread out across the floor. They do not sit in their assigned spots, but instead, are relaxed—lying down or reclining, leaning along the wall, haphazardly spaced around the room.

When Mrs. Tucker comes over to the meeting area, she begins to check the children's formations. These moments remind me of sectional rehearsals, during which musicians are able to practice and receive targeted feedback from the maestro about how to improve as individual players. On this particular day, the students are working on lowercase r, m, and n. Mrs. Tucker has been watching the students; they have practiced for several minutes as she walks around the room giving individual feedback and guidance. In the middle of the practice time, she requests everyone's attention for an announcement. "I don't want to focus too much on this one, but I'm noticing some oopses."

After taking a moment to demonstrate the proper way of writing an r—"middle start, pull down, push around"—she turns to the mistakes she is noticing. "I want to say some great oopses I saw. I saw some of these." She draws an r near the top of the easel whiteboard, first drawing a vertical line, picking up her marker, then adding a small curve near the top. It is recognizable as an r. "That might look familiar to some of you. . . . And then I saw some of these." She draws an m, making two humps by moving her pen from right to left. "Can't start on this side," she says, putting an X through the letter she just drew, "so it's a great try, but it's down and around, down and around." She writes the letter r over and over, moving left to right, as the children join the chant. "Now, tell me what to do."

"Down and around, down and around," the class again chants together in chorus.

Mrs. Tucker sings, "*Where do you start your letters? At the . . .*"

"*Top top top!*" the students sing back to her in reply.

After continuing to demonstrate the *r, m,* and *n,* Mrs. Tucker resumes her walk around the room, offering feedback to the students, as needed, while they are practicing their letter writing.

"Not quite what I showed you." She stands behind Justin, puts her right hand over his, and guides his hand as she makes a letter on the board.

Looking at Edward's work with the correctly formed letters, she asks, "Did you have your Letter-*O*'s?"

"Russ, almost. You're making it harder than you have to, buddy." As she has just done with Justin, she guides Russ's hand in hers, as she recounts the steps to form the letter properly.

"Rachel, can I watch? Oop, oop, can you do . . . " She trails off into directions about how to do the letter.

As she meanders around the room talking to the children one on one, she makes her way over to observe Felix, who is still early in the process of learning his letters and letter sounds. He is making some progress, forming the letter in the sequence of lines the way she just demonstrated. "Aye-yai-yai, buddy. I'm so impressed." Mrs. Tucker continues to look on as he writes again, but he does not replicate the sequence. "Felix, you had it the first time. Don't trick yourself." She comes closer to him, bending down to take a look at his whiteboard. She gently takes the whiteboard and marker from him and holds his hand in hers as she models how to draw the letter. With each stroke of the marker, their hands move in sync—with this approach, Mrs. Tucker gives Felix the physical sensation of making the letter in the proper form. After her demonstration, she leaves him to continue practice on his own. In this sense, she has identified and made him aware of this mistake, done a kinesthetic reteach of how to do it, and left him to practice further. She steps away from Felix and continues to make her rounds.

Almost daily, the children are independently practicing their letters like this, with Mrs. Tucker's modeling and direct feedback in real time. As she says, sings, and chants reminders to them of what she has taught before, the interactions are followed immediately by additional practice. They have access to check in with her again when needed but working on whiteboards allows students to also have more control over their experience as they practice. "Once kids can admit that they're making mistakes, I can work with them so much more." She helps them to face those mistakes and to respond by trying again, rather than shutting down. One way this manifests is that many of their mistakes can simply be wiped away. I often observe Mrs. Tucker quickly smudge away a malformed or mistaken letter from one of the whiteboards.

- Wipes the board clean. "Let's do some of these together."
- "You go, girl." Wipes the board clean. "Woo woo woo."
- "You're on a roll now." Wipes the board clean.

Whether the student has just made a mistake and needs to try again or has just demonstrated knowing how to write it correctly, the response is to wipe away and either do it again or move on to the next learning task.

This example demonstrates one of many ways that Mrs. Tucker devotes time and effort to closely monitoring students as they work, offering specific feedback, circulating to see what they are doing, and intervening with questions or demonstrations to nudge them toward the expectations she holds for them. At the same time, she also structures the class so that students can do a lot of self-evaluation and have the freedom to make choices for themselves. This support of student self-checks starts first by promoting the idea that everyone is doing things in their own way, at an individually appropriate pace. She offers space for them to "experiment on their own and realize, 'You know what? It doesn't matter what Joe Schmoe's doing, . . . this is what's right for me.'" This is a priority for her. It is her goal to help her students do for themselves: "Primarily, I want to teach them to become their own little person, and I feel like the academics are so second or third in all of that." This rises above the focus on reading and writing—being independent and self-driven is number one. She demonstrates this through both explicit messaging and interjecting when events come up in the class.

When she is giving directions to the children about picking goals, she reminds them in advance to focus on identifying something that works specifically for them. "Whatever goal is just right for you is just right for you. But I don't want to hear someone say 'easy!'" She points to Francis, an older man who has volunteered with Mrs. Tucker for many years since his son was in her class long ago, and says, "Because maybe my friend Francis over there is thinking, that sounds kinda hard, and if someone says 'That's easy' out loud, he may be thinking, 'Oh no! They said it's easy. I should know how to do that.' Whatever's right for Francis is right for Francis; whatever's right for me is right for me." In this moment, she encourages the students to have confidence to make a call for themselves in order to identify what best meets their needs, to avoid worrying about what others are doing, and to be discreet, so as not to discourage class-mates who may be at different levels from them, while also fostering empathy for how their friends might be feeling.

Mrs. Tucker does the same in reference to the children's knowledge of addition problems. She acknowledges that for a problem like $3 + 6 = 9$, some students may have already memorized the fact family and can recall the answer from memory, as "snap math." At the same time, others in the class will still need to employ stretch math strategies, like adding together on their fingers, counting on, and so forth, in order to reach the solution. And in her view, "If that's snap math for you, that's fantastic. If it's not, that's okay—we can keep doing stretch math. That's okay." The point is not for everyone to do things in the exact same way, but for people to be aware of their own needs and respectful that the needs of others may be different from their own.

Having several teachers and volunteers in the room during indepen-dent writing really seems to make a big difference in providing the stu-dents with individual support for their writing. These extra adults can offer students private lessons that are tailored to their individual needs. This individual support and feedback help each child in the class to get what they need in order to improve their skill and perform well. During this time, Mrs. Tucker floats around, checking on one child after the other; and although she doesn't necessarily get to all of them, they all receive some attention either from her, her classroom aide, or one of the volunteers. In addition to any checks by the teacher or volunteers, the students also turn to their peers to check their work. At the end of their writing time, students get a check in their "buddy box." Everybody is able to get a check in their box because a partner has checked with them to make sure they are doing things right on their work. The buddy box comes from the curriculum they use and dictates that "when they write, they have to be able to read to someone." In Mrs. Tucker's view, "It's just sort of reminding them they need to explain it and be able to take owner-ship."

LEADING GREAT PERFORMANCES, "OOPSES" AND ALL

> I make a point of telling them that oopses are great and that you just
> made a fantastic mistake, 'cause look what you learned. . . . I purpose-
> ly make mistakes and highlight them, so the kids will also see that
> that's a good thing to just try things out.
> – Mrs. Tucker

Whether it is subtly in a hushed voice while leaning over a small table, co-examining a few lines of writing, or during the Catch My Oops game show with Bonkers, Mrs. Tucker's classroom message is clear: mistakes are meant to be seen. Mrs. Tucker believes that it is important to "always be respectful" of her students, taking care to "never address student errors in a way that's going to embarrass them." During my time in Mrs. Tucker's class, I witness her repeatedly replay and analyze the "fantastic oopses" that students make. Just as the orchestra conductor references the full musical score that includes the melodies and dynamics of every instrument, Mrs. Tucker references her knowledge of every students' abilities and of the content she is teaching. Mrs. Tucker cheers for mistakes, thanks the students for their mistakes, and congratulates her students for making mistakes. In her work with the students, she conveys that there is both an element of good, as well as practical utility, in taking time to look closely at mistakes.

When mistakes are made, Mrs. Tucker provides feedback, but also— within that safe space—allows whatever happens to unfold naturally and in community. When mistakes happen publicly, she takes the time to demonstrate in detail what is wrong. First, she slows the moment down, so the mistake is visible to everyone. Then they have a conversation about it; she often offers an explanation for why it makes sense that it happened. Next, she gives the person who made the mistake—or the class as a whole—the chance to pick out what is wrong for themselves. And finally, they are given a chance to correct it, followed by a reward or praise for the fact that the mistake happened. In her classroom, she orchestrates the children's learning and relies on their mistakes to keep the movement going forward. While the musicians in an orchestra play their individual parts, the conductor is monitoring the quality, timing, and timbre coming from the instruments to ensure that, as a collective, the notes synthesize into a beautiful sound. In the same manner, I, too, experience the beauty of watching Mrs. Tucker conduct student learning from mistakes in her class.

CONCLUSION

As I reflect upon my immersion into these four kindergarten classrooms, what strikes me the most is that they truly felt worlds apart from each other. I spent many hundreds of hours observing these teachers—first in person and in real time, and then later by closely reviewing videos of thousands of micro-level, teacher-student interactions. Through this process, a whole new perspective opened to me, and the evidence tangibly demonstrates the extent to which contextual factors impact the small moments of day-to-day instruction and learning from mistakes in kindergarten. I find it particularly striking that within just a fifteen-mile radius, children can have such radically different learning experiences with their teachers and peers.

Upon comparison, I found that these four teachers frame mistakes very distinctly from each other. In Mr. Allen's class, mistakes are defined by the standards enacted by the district—benchmarks that his students must meet before the close of the school year. He works to advance students toward satisfactory performance on various assessments, while divulging to me on multiple occasions that the projected goals feel daunting, if not impossible, to meet for all of his students. Mr. Allen functions in a context with extremely constrained resources—namely, lack of financial, instructional, and familial support—and is only able to provide limited academic feedback to children. He does the best job he can with the formidable constraints and scarcity that define his daily classroom instruction. In the mistake culture of his classroom, he readily accepts students' incorrect attempts, meeting them where they are by acknowledging their partially correct answers and leading them toward the right responses soon after.

When it comes to mistakes, the children in Miss Carrie's class are in the driver's seat, with the teacher serving as their supportive guide, providing indirect and direct scaffolding so they can succeed. It is fascinating that within her child-centered, Montessori approach, Miss Carrie is somehow completely in control of children's experiences, while simultaneously not in control at all. The children interact with Miss Carrie at check-ins, when she might tell them that they are making a mistake or that their work is correct. However, mistakes in her class are related to each student's own self-assessment. Often, her efforts are more about supporting children so they can figure out right answers for themselves, urging them to check their work repeatedly until all the pieces fit together as designated by the directions for using the materials. While there is a specific way the children must complete the "works" that they select, they own the process and often have the answers at their disposal at all times, which they can check afterward.

Ms. Rivers is similar to Miss Carrie in that the line between right and wrong is crisp. There is not a halfway correct answer; the children are either 100 percent right or have more work to do in order to correct the answer and move forward. However, unlike Miss Carrie who requires children to independently self-correct and conducts most of her feedback on mistakes with one or two children at a time, Ms. Rivers takes a whole-group approach to teaching in general and correcting mistakes specifically. Further, Ms. Rivers is bold in the way she directly calls out mistakes and drives very hard toward specific, right answers—arguably giving feedback that is even harsher than most adults would be accustomed to receiving. Her methods compel kindergarten students to sustain focus on academic work for the duration of a very long school day. In addition, little attention is given to children's individual emotions; instead, focus is pushed squarely onto the purpose of being in the room: to reach a high and measurable academic performance. This manifests as a steadfast pursuit of fully right answers. When Ms. Rivers is with the whole group, she leverages everyone's brainpower to draw toward the "perfect perfect" answer, declining to validate any of the partially correct answers along the way. The emphasis on achievement does seem to translate into academic success on tests given to her kindergarten children; however, it is difficult to calculate the cost of driving young learners so hard.

In a suburban school on the other side of the city, Mrs. Tucker has a diametrically opposed approach to that of Ms. Rivers. Although there are clearly right and wrong answers in her class, Mrs. Tucker frequently shares and celebrates student mistakes, rather than swiftly rooting them out and moving past them. That is not to say that she does not consistently correct children when they make errors and provide necessary corrective feedback for improvement. However, there are times when the children make mistakes that she readily accepts and expects, given their developmental level, and she actually calls the class to attention, claps her hands in celebration, and thanks the student for making the mistake. Mrs. Tucker tries to leverage these mistake moments, offering a means by which to address challenges that the children can anticipate in the future. She often shifts the blame away from them and onto external others—for example, the designers of the English language; the letters that flipped themselves backward—thereby mitigating the responsibility for the students' mistakes. While Mrs. Tucker is adamant that children work toward right answers on the provided activities, she simultaneously differentiates instruction so that expectations increase as abilities advance and are scaled back for students who would benefit from a slower pace.

As we look at these four teachers, the mistake culture within each classroom is distinctive, with varied interactional practices, language, tone of voice, and nonverbal cues. Although these four teachers respond to mistakes very differently, I identified some throughlines that emerged across settings. If I had the opportunity to invite these teachers into the same room, I think a lot of their big-picture, high-level ideas about kindergarten instruction would align: their understanding of the developmental abilities of young children; their grasp of the general range of content that is typically introduced in kindergarten; and the importance of establishing a classroom community and of encouraging children to do their own thinking and their own work.

The greatest link I observed across all four teachers is that mistakes play a central role in how they facilitate classroom dynamics and day-to-day instruction. Whether it is driving hard toward 100 percent correct articulations of answers and insights in Ms. Rivers's class, or referencing the right answer to check a work in Miss Carrie's Montessori class, these four teachers work while having particular learning strategies and correct answers in mind. The types of scaffolding that they provide, the quality of educational activities that they lead, and the variety of ways that they interact and communicate with the children are different, but the importance of mistakes in the learning process is crystal clear in each classroom.

At the same time, these teachers recognize that mistakes are an inevitable part of kindergarten. All four drew the children's attention to tricky spellings and explained how some English words do not align with their pronunciations. All four shared with me at some point that mistakes definitely happen in kindergarten and that they happen repeatedly, all day. All four acknowledged that the children's developmental level at the start of the year reflected their limited exposure to classroom processes and that, at first, they would likely not know how to maintain focus, engage in discussion, or work independently. But the teachers also felt that over the arc of the year, they could really help children make great strides in these areas.

Despite this handful of surface-level alignments, I found substantial and quite stunning differences once I drilled down and looked frame by frame at the day-to-day work and interactions of each teacher and classroom community. The teachers' circumstances and the expectations set in their respective schools offer a variety of constraints and affordances. Looking across the four classrooms, I witnessed firsthand how teachers' access to resources, prevailing theories of learning, philosophies about the role of mistakes in learning, and the choice of words, affect, and nonverbal communication necessarily shape how they interact with their kindergarten students. Also, other important factors outside of their classroom—for example, school culture, district-mandated standards and assessments, financial resources that fund materials and support staff, level of parental involvement—play a key role in motivating particular types of instructional moves, at the micro-level and beyond. Even with intentional and thoughtful instruction, these featured veteran teachers—as well as many others—might not realize the extent to which their practices differ from the classroom next door, down the road, or across town.

Each of these four teachers presents a slightly different perspective on mistakes in kindergarten. As deduced from the teacher-student interactions I observed, they run along a gradient of mistake tolerance that colors how mishaps and misunderstandings are couched in the class: from an unacceptable inconvenience, to a mundane day-to-day occurrence, to an exciting opportunity. Ms. Rivers emphasizes that children should doggedly pursue the precisely correct answer by paying close attention, staying focused, and taking care to eliminate—or better yet, avoid—mistakes. She sticks with challenging learning for long stretches of time to help the kindergarteners on her team quickly identify the exact right answers and then explain their rationale for the answers. She praises children when their self-determination pays off and they do get the right articulation. But any partially incorrect answers or lapses of focus are frowned upon. The message I receive from Ms. Rivers's approach is that mistakes are intolerable and in opposition to learning. The team's job is to urgently arrive at perfect performance, improving individual students' skills so they can obtain right answers quickly and easily to help the group learn.

Mr. Allen and Miss Carrie are somewhat neutral in their tolerance of student mistakes. Although they want children to make their way to the right answer, and they work to ensure that their students eventually get to them (in different ways), both of these teachers very clearly accept mistakes as natural occurrences throughout the day; they do not tend to get particularly charged up about them. Out of the four teachers, these two are perhaps the most inclined to give a child the right answer when really stumped—for example, when Miss Carrie tells children the word they are attempting to sound out, or when Mr. Allen reveals the correct letter sound as the girls playing ABC Bingo repeatedly make errors. In both contexts, I feel the primary message conveyed to the children is that mistakes are no big deal—they are expected and normal. When mistakes happen, these teachers expect that children should just continue moving forward and try their best to correct them.

Mrs. Tucker—compared to Ms. Rivers—is at the other end of the spectrum. While she does take care to provide corrective feedback when appropriate, she also actively cheers when the children make mistakes. Mrs. Tucker seems most enthusiastic if it happens in whole group and excitedly calls for the attention of the other children to go through a demonstration of why the mistake was logical and what the right answer is. She even goes so far as to give rewards for some "oopses" and thanks the child. When her kindergarteners stop making mistakes or skills become too easy for them, Mrs. Tucker sees this as a transitional moment, positioned as a marker of time to move to the next level in their learning. As she says, "You're getting smarter; I'm getting harder." A key takeaway from her classroom is that mistakes are information—they help us to understand where a learner is in their development and can be used to devise a strategy to help advance learning.

The actual process of correcting mistakes also varies across these four classrooms. Miss Carrie in her Montessori class and Ms. Rivers in her charter school are willing to stick with students for quite a long time, until they can figure out how to self-adjust and correct their answers. Miss Carrie essentially floats from student to student, as needed, because the children work independently in her class almost all the time. Daily teacher check-ins are relatively rare for individual students; but from the teacher perspective, Miss Carrie spends virtually all her instructional time in interactions with one to two students. Ms. Rivers keeps the students together in a block or team for almost all of the instructional time, with very limited individual check-ins with children. But in both cases, once they are working with a student or with the class to solve a problem, the children are expected to keep trying until they reach the answer. Although the Montessori and charter school classrooms run at different speeds and in tremendously disparate formats, both settings offer a similar aim, in that there is no way to sidestep or opt out of participation in classroom learning. Children cannot simply sit to the side and wait for the teacher to eventually just tell them the right answer. In the end, the onus lies with the children. By contrast, Mrs. Tucker and Mr. Allen push much more quickly through wrong answers, providing clues to the answer that end up helping children easily correct and move past mistakes. This makes sense given the orientation of the schools. Mrs. Tucker is committed to following a rigid district-wide curriculum that requires the class to move through at a certain pace, along with all other kindergarten teachers in the district. Mr. Allen feels like he is under constant pressure to get his underperforming students to catch up to district-wide benchmarks, as demonstrated on a litany of assessments; he also has scant one-on-one time for feedback given the dense schedule of specials and lack of personnel to support his instructional goals.

Beyond comparing the nuts and bolts of how each of these veteran teachers handle mistakes in their instructional practice, I think the role of affect during academic-centered corrective feedback is one of the most noteworthy differences I observed in these classes. This is evidenced by each teachers' tone of voice and nonverbal communication. When it comes to behaviors, I saw all of the teachers use iterations of a stern countenance in their classroom management—a flat tone to tell a child to stop a particular action; a smile turned to a straight face or a frown in response to inattention or unkind behavior; an eyebrow furrowed when children talk over directions. As it pertains to academic mistakes, all four say the words "I disagree" to some extent in their classrooms. When they do so, Mr. Allen, Miss Carrie, and Mrs. Tucker typically use a "sing-song" or upbeat tone to make the statement, providing a pleasant-sounding counter to the children's incorrect answers. The direction and content of the feedback is clear, but in timbre, it sounds fairly similar to when they say "I agree" or offer other positive displays of agreement to the children. However, Ms. Rivers very frequently uses a negative tone to express that an answer to an academic question is wrong. While all the teachers offer corrective feedback that directly counters children's mistakes and labels them as incorrect, Ms. Rivers conveys her frustration and disappointment in a manner that I did not observe during my time in the other classrooms.

The juxtaposition of these four public-school kindergarten teachers lays bare the extent to which responses to mistakes vary across these kindergarten contexts. Each teacher operates in a particular set of circumstances—some aspects fall within their control, but others are beyond the realm of what they can change or manipulate on their own. Whether or not they respond actively or passively, teachers make choices about how they talk to students about their mistakes, when they provide corrective feedback, and what emotional information they share during teacher-child interactions.

Knowing this, what should we do? How can teachers, parents, administrators, and policy makers take action to positively impact the mistake culture of classrooms in U.S. schools and beyond? I think that our course of action should be threefold. First, we can take the time to consider what we, as individuals, currently do in our interactions with others—in schools, in the workplace, at home, or otherwise. Whether we attend to it or not, we have habits and patterns of behavior that typify our responses to mistakes and influence those around us. How would you articulate your personal philosophy about mistakes in the classroom? What, if any, adjustments do you aspire to make? How do your responses to mistakes and feedback vary across the different contexts of your life? By taking a step back to examine our own practices and life experiences through the lens of these portraits, we have an opportunity to foster a deeper appreciation for the ways we impact others through our responses. If inspired, surprised, or appalled by the circumstances or actions of the four teachers, we can decide what we want to strive for as we frame or reframe mistakes for ourselves and others.

Second, these portraits remind us that the ways people interact with each other and navigate the world—including how teachers engage their students—are necessarily shaped by the contextual factors in which they are immersed. It is worth noting that these teachers encountered wide variations in circumstances while teaching young children in early childhood settings. I imagine that if resource levels, supports, or external pressures were shifted, these four teachers might respond to their students' mistakes in a different manner. When considering potential behaviors of teachers and students beyond the kindergarten grade level and in various content areas, I can only imagine the diversity of micro-level responses to mistakes that we might detect. More importantly, when we consider the ways in which U.S. schools and districts differ across zip codes and by the median household income of the surrounding neighborhoods, responses to mistakes within a single metropolitan area may emerge as a tangible manifestation of a broader equity issue. Just across these four cases we can see that inequitable access to resources impacts day-to-day classroom teaching, resulting in differences in the ways both teachers and students respond to mistakes.

And third, this collection of portraits illustrates that learning and teaching from mistakes is multifaceted and includes elements beyond academics. Instruction not only includes aspects of pedagogy, planning, and resources, but also necessarily is a human endeavor that manifests in how people—including kindergarten teachers and their students—relate to each other through communication in the context of relationship. Teachers do not speak to their students by telling them district standards and target test scores, but through nuanced yet meaningful, verbal conversations, nonverbal gestures, actions, and class mottos, as well as through implicitly and explicitly stated rules and expectations. This is high stakes, and teachers should tread carefully in this space. Although we should certainly focus on the good work of helping children learn and of building a foundation for their future, moment by moment, we also are molding young children's mindsets, their orientation toward learning, and their trust toward schools and teachers in ways that could have a broader impact on how they will navigate their entire K–12 academic careers.

With so much responsibility, I hope that we can be more aware of and intentional about the ways we respond to students' mistakes. Beyond trying to emulate one of these veteran teachers as a role model, or simply cherry-picking our favorite strategies that we might want to try out from these four portraits, we can choose to take a more robust approach to honing our practices in this important arena. Rather than aiming to get our responses to mistakes "just right," let us instead think about how we can develop practices that foster ongoing self-reflection and that help us make adjustments across contexts, communities, and the passage of time. May we become aware of the subtle attributes of the mistake cultures in which we are presently engaged and appreciate how feedback and mistakes impact our students, workplaces, and lives—as complex, messy, emotional, and human as they may be.

SELECTED BIBLIOGRAPHY

Anyon, J. (1980). Social class and the hidden curriculum of work. *Journal of Education, 162*(1), 67–92.

Bereiter, C., & Scardamalia, M. (1993). *Surpassing ourselves: An inquiry into and implications of expertise.* Open Court.

Borasi, R. (1994). Capitalizing on errors as "springboards for inquiry": A teaching experiment. *Journal for Research in Mathematics Education, 25*(2), 166–208.

Bray, W. S. (2011). A collective case study of the influence of teachers' beliefs and knowledge on error-handling practices during class discussion of mathematics. *Journal for Research in Mathematics Education, 42*(1), 2–38.

Brooker, R. J., Buss, K. A., & Dennis, T. A. (2011). Error-monitoring brain activity is associated with affective behaviors in young children. *Developmental Cognitive Neuroscience, 1*(2), 141–152.

Charmaz, K. (2006). *Constructing grounded theory: A practical guide through qualitative analysis.* Sage.

Clare, L., & Jones, R. S. (2008). Errorless learning in the rehabilitation of memory impairment: A critical review. *Neuropsychology Review, 18*(1), 1–23.

D'Mello, S., Lehman, B., Pekrun, R., & Graesser, A. (2012). Confusion can be beneficial for learning. *Learning and Instruction, 29*, 153–170.

Donaldson, M. (2019). Harnessing the power of fantastic attempts: Kindergarten teacher perspectives on children's mistakes. *Journal of Educational Research, 112*(4), 535–549.

Donaldson, M. (2019). Teacher accounts of children's mistakes in the kindergarten classroom. *Journal of Ethnographic and Qualitative Research, 13*(3), 187–197.

Donaldson, M. (2020). "Everything go upside down": Navigating mistakes in early learning and teaching. *Schools: Studies in Education, 17*(1), 70–91.

Donaldson, M. (2020). Tools to build their best learning: Examining how kindergarten teachers frame student mistakes. *Harvard Educational Review, 90*(1), 54–74.

Duckworth, A. L., Peterson, C., Matthews, M. D., & Kelly, D. R. (2007). Grit: Perseverance and passion for long-term goals. *Journal of Personality and Social Psychology, 92*(6), 1087–1101.

Dweck, C. (2006). *Mindset: The new psychology of success.* Random House.

Emerson, R. M., Fretz, R. I., & Shaw, L. L. (1995). *Writing ethnographic fieldnotes.* University of Chicago Press.

Finn, B., & Metcalfe, J. (2010). Scaffolding feedback to maximize long-term error correction. *Memory & Cognition, 38*(7), 951–961.

Fredrickson, B. L. (2001). The role of positive emotions in positive psychology: The broaden-and-build theory of positive emotions. *The American Psychologist, 56*(3), 218–226.

Geertz, C. (1973). *The interpretation of cultures: Selected essays.* Basic Books.

Gehring, W. J., Goss, B., Coles, M. G., Meyer, D. E., & Donchin, E. (1993). A neural system for error detection and compensation. *Psychological Science, 4*(6), 385–390.

Graesser, A. C., & D'Mello, S. (2012). Emotions during the learning of difficult material. In B. Ross (Ed.), *The Psychology of Learning and Motivation* (Vol. 57, pp. 183–225). Elsevier.

Hajcak, G. (2012). What we've learned from mistakes: Insights from error-related brain activity. *Current Directions in Psychological Science, 21*(2), 101–106.

Hattie, J., & Timperley, H. (2007). The power of feedback. *Review of Educational Research, 77*(1), 81–112.

Heinze, A. (2005). Mistake-handling activities in the mathematics classroom. In H. L. Chick & J. L. Vincent (Eds.), *Proceedings of the 29th Conference of the International Group for the Psychology of Mathematics Education* (Vol. 3, pp. 105–112). PME.

Holroyd, C. B., & Coles, M. G. (2002). The neural basis of human error processing: Reinforcement learning, dopamine, and the error-related negativity. *Psychological Review, 109*(4), 679–709.

Huelser, B. J., & Metcalfe, J. (2012). Making related errors facilitates learning, but learners do not know it. *Memory & Cognition, 40*(4), 1–14.

Immordino-Yang, M. H., & Damasio, A. (2007). We feel, therefore we learn: The relevance of affective and social neuroscience to education. *Mind, Brain, and Education, 1*(1), 3–10.

Kang, S. H., Pashler, H., Cepeda, N. J., Rohrer, D., Carpenter, S. K., & Mozer, M. C. (2011). Does incorrect guessing impair fact learning? *Journal of Educational Psychology, 103*(1), 48–59.

Kornell, N., Hays, M. J., & Bjork, R. A. (2009). Unsuccessful retrieval attempts enhance subsequent learning. *Journal of Experimental Psychology: Learning, Memory, and Cognition, 35*(4), 989–998.

Lareau, A. (2002). Invisible inequality: Social class and childrearing in Black families and White families. *American Sociological Review, 67*(5), 747–776.

Lawrence-Lightfoot, S., & Davis, J. H. (1997). *The art and science of portraiture.* Jossey-Bass.

Lemov, D. (2010). *Teach like a champion: 49 techniques that put students on the path to college.* Jossey-Bass.

Lewis, M., Takai-Kawakami, K., Kawakami, K., & Sullivan, M. W. (2010). Cultural differences in emotional responses to success and failure. *International Journal of Behavioral Development, 34*(1), 53–61.

Light, R. J., Singer, J. D., & Willett, J. B (1990). *By design: Planning research on higher education.* Harvard University Press.

Lottero-Perdue, P. S., & Parry, E. A. (2017). Perspectives on failure in the classroom by elementary teachers new to teaching engineering. *Journal of Pre-College Engineering Education Research (J-PEER), 7*(1), 47–67.

Metcalfe, J., & Finn, B. (2012). Hypercorrection of high confidence errors in children. *Learning and Instruction, 22*(4), 253–261.

Metcalfe, J., & Kornell, N. (2007). Principles of cognitive science in education: The effects of generation, errors, and feedback. *Psychonomic Bulletin & Review, 14*(2), 225–229.

Metcalfe, J., Kornell, N., & Finn, B. (2009). Delayed versus immediate feedback in children's and adults' vocabulary learning. *Memory & Cognition, 37*(8), 1077–1087.

Meyer, A., Weinberg, A., Klein, D. N., & Hajcak, G. (2012). The development of the error-related negativity (ERN) and its relationship with anxiety: Evidence from 8 to 13 year-olds. *Developmental Cognitive Neuroscience, 2*(1), 152–162.

Miles, M. B., & Huberman, A. M. (1994). *Qualitative data analysis: An expanded sourcebook.* Sage.

Palermo, F., Hanish, L. D., Martin, C. L., Fabes, R. A., & Reiser, M. (2007). Preschoolers' academic readiness: What role does the teacher-child relationship play? *Early Childhood Research Quarterly, 22*(4), 407–422.

Pashler, H., Cepeda, N. J., Wixted, J. T., & Rohrer, D. (2005). When does feedback facilitate learning of words? *Journal of Experimental Psychology: Learning, Memory, and Cognition, 31*(1), 3–8.

Pashler, H., Rohrer, D., Cepeda, N. J., & Carpenter, S. K. (2007). Enhancing learning and retarding forgetting: Choices and consequences. *Psychonomic Bulletin & Review*, *14*(2), 187–193.

Pianta, R. C., Hamre, B., & Stuhlman, M. (2003). Relationships between teachers and children. In I. B. Weiner (Ed.), *Handbook of Psychology* (pp. 199–234). John Wiley.

Ryan, R. M., & Deci, E. L. (2000). Self-determination theory and the facilitation of intrinsic motivation, social development, and well-being. *American Psychologist*, *55*(1), 68–78.

Rybowiak, V., Garst, H., Frese, M., & Batinic, B. (1999). Error orientation questionnaire (EOQ): Reliability, validity, and different language equivalence. *Journal of Organizational Behavior*, *20*(4), 527–547.

Santagata, R. (2004). "Are you joking or are you sleeping?" Cultural beliefs and practices in Italian and U.S. teachers' mistake-handling strategies. *Linguistics and Education*, *15*(1–2), 141–164.

Santagata, R. (2005). Practices and beliefs in mistake-handling activities: A video study of Italian and U.S. mathematics lessons. *Teaching and Teacher Education*, *21*(5), 491–508.

Schleppenbach, M., Flevares, L. M., Sims, L. M., & Perry, M. (2007). Teachers' responses to student mistakes in Chinese and U.S. mathematics classrooms. *Elementary School Journal*, *108*(2), 131–147.

Seidman, I. (2006). *Interviewing as qualitative research: A guide for researchers in education and the social sciences* (3rd ed.). Teachers College Press.

Seifried, J., & Wuttke, E. (2010). Student errors: How teachers diagnose and respond to them. *Empirical Research in Vocational Education and Training*, *2*(2), 147–162.

Steuer, G., & Dresel, M. (2015). A constructive error climate as an element of effective learning environments. *Psychological Test and Assessment Modeling*, *57*(2), 262–275.

Strauss, A., & Corbin, J. (1994). Grounded theory methodology: An overview. In N. K. Denzin (Ed.), *Handbook of qualitative research* (pp. 273–285). Sage.

Taylor, S. F., Stern, E. R., & Gehring, W. J. (2007). Neural systems for error monitoring: Recent findings and theoretical perspectives. *The Neuroscientist*, *13*(2), 160–172.

Tomaka, J., Blascovich, J., Kibler, J., & Ernst, J. M. (1997). Cognitive and physiological antecedents of threat and challenge appraisal. *Journal of Personality and Social Psychology*, *73*(1), 63–72.

Torpey, D. C., Hajcak, G., & Klein, D. N. (2009). An examination of error-related brain activity and its modulation by error value in young children. *Developmental Neuropsychology*, *34*(6), 749–761.

Tulis, M. (2013). Error management behavior in classrooms: Teachers' responses to student mistakes. *Teaching and Teacher Education*, *33*(1), 56–68.

Vygotsky, L. S. (1980). Interaction between learning and development. In M. Cole, V. John-Steiner, S. Scribner, & E. Souberman (Eds.), *Mind in society: The development of higher psychological processes* (pp. 79–91). Harvard University Press.

Zentall, S. R., & Morris, B. J. (2010). "Good job, you're so smart": The effects of inconsistency of praise type on young children's motivation. *Journal of Experimental Child Psychology*, *107*(2), 155–163.

Zentall, S., & Morris, B. (2012). A critical eye: Praise directed toward traits increases children's eye fixations on errors and decreases motivation. *Psychonomic Bulletin & Review*, *19*(6), 1073–1077.

ACKNOWLEDGMENTS

Many wonderful people supported me as I completed this book, which I began during my doctoral program at Harvard and finished in my first years as an assistant professor. First, I would like to sincerely thank my dissertation committee (Tina Grotzer, Sara Lawrence-Lightfoot, and Kitty Boles), my writing group (Amy Cheung, Stuti Shukla, Lynneth Solis, and Tori Theisen-Homer), and my long-time Project Zero lab mates (Shane Tutwiler and Megan Powell Cuzzolino) for their substantive feedback on so many ideas and drafts over the years, as well as the motivation to just keep writing. I am also grateful for the many professors and mentors at the Harvard Graduate School of Education who taught, supported, and believed in me over the years, with special thanks to John Willett.

Next, I thank the family and friends in my life who walked through the journey with me and cheered me on during the highs and lows along the way. I am forever indebted to my mother, Cynthia Norfleet Donaldson, for her continuous love, willingness to listen, confidence in me, and copy-editing prowess. I thank my beloved daughter, Naomi Gramling, for being a fire in my heart as I have pursued this work and for her patience as I worked on this project throughout many of her own early years. I also must express my appreciation for the wide and wonderful circle of friends who have walked through this journey with me and surrounded me with love, care, and confidence that assured me I could do this even when it was hard. Extra thanks to Aubry Threlkeld, Ashley Jungjohan, Elizabeth Gramling, Rebecca Gramling, Rachel Moo, and Jim Zartman for their continued, enthusiastic, and robust support along the way.

This work was funded in part by the American Educational Research Association, the Center on the Developing Child (Harvard University), and the Institute for Translational Research (University of Hartford). Sincere thanks to these organizations for providing fellowships and grants in support of this study when it was still under development.

Finally, I must express my deep appreciation for the children, teachers, and schools who inspired and informed this project. I am grateful to my kindergarten students from years ago whose responses to mistakes and feedback sparked the questions that I have explored in these portraits. Endless thanks to the four teachers who so graciously opened their classrooms to me, trusting me to join their class community for a time and to tell their stories to the world. It is my honor to bring to light their experiences with mistakes and learning so that future kindergarteners and their teachers will benefit from the lessons revealed in this volume.